The Coral Way Bilingual Program

BILINGUAL EDUCATION & BILINGUALISM

Series Editors: Nancy H. Hornberger *(University of Pennsylvania, USA)* and Wayne E. Wright *(Purdue University, USA)*

Bilingual Education and Bilingualism is an international, multidisciplinary series publishing research on the philosophy, politics, policy, provision and practice of language planning, indigenous and minority language education, multilingualism, multiculturalism, biliteracy, bilingualism and bilingual education. The series aims to mirror current debates and discussions. New proposals for single-authored, multiple-authored or edited books in the series are warmly welcomed in any of the following categories or others authors may propose: overview or introductory texts; course readers or general reference texts; focus books on particular multilingual education program types; school-based case studies; national case studies; collected cases with a clear programmatic or conceptual theme; and professional education manuals.

All books in this series are externally peer-reviewed.

Full details of all the books in this series and of all our other publications can be found on http://www.multilingual-matters.com, or by writing to Multilingual Matters, St Nicholas House, 31-34 High Street, Bristol BS1 2AW, UK.

BILINGUAL EDUCATION & BILINGUALISM: 120

The Coral Way Bilingual Program

Maria R. Coady

MULTILINGUAL MATTERS
Bristol • Blue Ridge Summit

DOI https://doi.org/10.21832/COADY4573
Library of Congress Cataloging in Publication Data
A catalog record for this book is available from the Library of Congress.
Names: Coady, Maria R., author.
Title: The Coral Way Bilingual Program/Maria R. Coady.
Description: Bristol, UK; Blue Ridge Summit, PA: Multilingual Matters, 2020. | Series:
   Bilingual education & Bilingualism: 120 | Includes bibliographical references and
   index. | Summary: "This book introduces readers to the first publicly funded, two-way
   bilingual program in the United States, Coral Way Elementary School. It provides
   an accurate, clear and accessible examination of the program, its historical, social
   and political origins, its successes and its relevance for future bilingual programs"—
   Provided by publisher.
Identifiers: LCCN 2019029671 (print) | LCCN 2019029672 (ebook) | ISBN 9781788924573
   (hardback) | ISBN 9781788924566 (paperback) | ISBN 9781788924580 (pdf) |
   ISBN 9781788924597 (epub) | ISBN 9781788924603 (kindle edition)
Subjects: LCSH: Education, Bilingual—Florida—Miami. | Education, Elementary—
   Florida—Miami. | Coral Way K-8 Center (Miami, Fla.)
Classification: LCC LC3733.M5 C63 2020 (print) | LCC LC3733.M5 (ebook) |
   DDC 370.11709759/381—dc23
LC record available at https://lccn.loc.gov/2019029671
LC ebook record available at https://lccn.loc.gov/2019029672

British Library Cataloguing in Publication Data
A catalogue entry for this book is available from the British Library.

ISBN-13: 978-1-78892-457-3 (hbk)
ISBN-13: 978-1-78892-456-6 (pbk)

Multilingual Matters
UK: St Nicholas House, 31-34 High Street, Bristol BS1 2AW, UK.
USA: NBN, Blue Ridge Summit, PA, USA.

Website: www.multilingual-matters.com
Twitter: Multi_Ling_Mat
Facebook: https://www.facebook.com/multilingualmatters
Blog: www.channelviewpublications.wordpress.com

The policy of Multilingual Matters/Channel View Publications is to use papers that
are natural, renewable and recyclable products, made from wood grown in sustainable
forests. In the manufacturing process of our books, and to further support our policy,
preference is given to printers that have FSC and PEFC Chain of Custody certification.
The FSC and/or PEFC logos will appear on those books where full certification has been
granted to the printer concerned.

Typeset by Deanta Global Publishing Services, Chennai, India.
Printed and bound in the UK by the CPI Books Group Ltd
Printed and bound in the US by NBN.

Contents

Acknowledgements

This book has been a sheer joy to write. Listening to the stories of former bilingual educators and their commitment to Coral Way has rejuvenated my advocacy for bilingual education, particularly in today's increasingly restrictive sociopolitical environment. I also believe that as we get older, we increasingly realize how important the past is. Thus, for me, writing *The Coral Way Bilingual Program* has been a journey that transcended time – from past to present and into the future.

First and foremost, I wish to thank Richard Ruiz who began the work on Coral Way in the late 2000s and whose inspiration and contribution to bilingual education in the United States cannot be underestimated. Alongside Richard, I wish to thank Bess de Farber, a colleague and now friend, who approached me with this work and who trusted me with the words and experiences of the former teachers of Coral Way between 1963 and 1968. I also wish to thank the former students and current educators of Coral Way who agreed to participate in this ongoing, longitudinal work. Their names are speckled throughout this book, but I especially wish to note Susana Martín from the Coral Way K-8 Bilingual Center who helped me gain access to the school and teachers. She is a true champion for bilingual education.

Others who have supported this work over the past two years include Dr Rosie Castro Feinberg, Dr Deon Heffington, Shuzhan Li, Andrew Long, Dr Mark Preston Lopez, Nidza Marichal, Aleksandra Olszewska, and Dr Lourdes Rovira who shared her wisdom and stories. The University of Florida librarians Brittany Kester and Perry Collins in the digital collections are simply amazing and assisted with obtaining permissions for use of archival data. Thank you to the Ford Foundation whose archives, approximately 280 pages, were accessed from the Rockefeller Archive Center in New York.

I also thank the series editors Dr Nancy Hornberger and Dr Wayne Wright who agreed that Coral Way was a story worth telling. To that end, Tommi Grover, Laura Longworth, Sarah Williams and Flo McClelland from the Multilingual Matters team also provided the best professional support an author could ask for. Multilingual Matters is a true ally in bilingual education worldwide.

My husband Tom, daughter Rae, stepchildren Austin and Emily, and pup Nori were willing to listen to me mumble around the house as I wrote and spoke endlessly about this exciting project. Rae provided professional graphic design support for the book cover and for reproduction of original materials in the book – thank you! Finally, this work is dedicated to my son, Thomas, whose absence from my life is ever present, a reminder that life is precious, and that although time passes by, we are forever changed by those who share our journey.

Foreword

I left my home country of Cuba on 22 July 1961, at the age of 9. Fortunately, I came with my parents and two brothers (ages 11 and 1), a luxury many other children did not enjoy, having to come by themselves through the Peter Pan initiative. The 22 July was to become a day of mixed emotions for our family; it was my father's birthday, my parents wedding anniversary and the day I said goodbye to everything I had known up to then.

In Miami, I was enrolled in a Catholic school where no special help was provided to the tens of Cuban students entering on a daily basis. However, I had attended The Phillips School in Cuba, a school owned by a Canadian couple where we had the morning session in English and the afternoon session in Spanish; thus, I had some knowledge of English. What I never foresaw as I started fifth grade in Miami is that throughout my teenage years I would sacrifice knowledge of my home language to join the bandwagon of the 1960s generation. I eventually graduated from the University of Miami in 1973 with limited academic Spanish and a degree in elementary education, at a time when teachers were a dime a dozen.

I recall sitting at home fully dressed and ready to leave on a minute's notice as I called school after school asking if they had a teaching position. Remember, we didn't even have faxes at the time! One 'no after another' scared me, until a clerk who answered the phone asked if I was bilingual. A very emphatic 'yes' got me an interview at Coral Way Elementary, a school about which I knew nothing.

I was hired to teach the English block to a fourth-grade group of students, but fate always takes its turns and two days before starting school, a teacher had emergency surgery and my assignment was changed to one block of English and one block of Spanish. My first day as a Spanish teacher at Coral Way was a turning point in my personal and professional life. Within the first 20 minutes of the school day, I had already written a huge mistake on the board to be quickly corrected by a student who not only pointed out my spelling mistake but gave me the grammatical rule for what I had done. Convinced that I was about to lose my job, as soon as school was dismissed, I drove to the only bookstore that sold Spanish books and bought every third-, fourth- and fifth-grade language book that I could find. When I got home, I had to sit through enough 'I told you so' from my mother who had insisted that we speak and study Spanish. There began my journey into the world of bilingualism, language and identity. I started studying Spanish to reappropriate myself with the language and culture I had lost.

Although I did not attend Coral Way Elementary as a student, Coral Way Elementary transformed my life. It took me from writing 'lapizes' with a 'z' on the board to becoming passionate about the Coral Way experience and an advocate for dual-language education. Little did I know that September day in 1973 that I would one day be the director of bilingual and world language education in Miami-Dade County Public Schools and, in 2009, be awarded the Cruz de Oficial de la Orden de Isabel la Católica for my work on behalf of the promotion of the Spanish language in the United States.

My experience is not unique. For hundreds of students that were fortunate to attend Coral Way, both English and Spanish speakers, their elementary experience was unlike any other at the time. Half a day in English, half a day in Spanish, 'acentos, diéresis', schwa sound, long vowels, square dancing one day and the cha cha cha the next during PE class. Students were exposed to two languages, two cultures and two different ways of reading the world.

Although Coral Way was to shape the landscape of bilingual education in the United States in the 20th century, little has been written about this transformative school with its Mediterranean architecture and beautiful central patio. For those who are immersed in the world of bilingual education, Coral Way Elementary (now Coral Way K-8 Center) is no stranger. However, what Coral Way contributed, and continues to contribute to the educational arena is worthy of being shouted from a mountain top (disseminated across the world).

Dr Maria Coady has done just that. With the publication of *The Coral Way Bilingual Program*, Dr Coady takes us on a journey from gestation and birth in the early 1960s to present-day implementation 56 years later. We learn that at the root of the Coral Way experiment was the Cuban exodus caused by the Castro revolution. We are introduced to the visionaries who dared to dream and challenge the establishment at a time when bilingual education was unheard of in a public school: Pauline Rojas, Paul Bell, Ralph Robinett, Joe Hall, Rosa Guas Inclán, Lee Logan and 'the Marines', the teachers, the trailblazers who 'bajo capa y espada' (against all odds...) made sure that the program was implemented with fidelity.

Dr Coady's book provides detailed descriptions and an in-depth study of the Coral Way program never before compiled under one cover. Her research is exhaustive and includes the political climate of Miami in the early years of the Cuban exodus, including the Peter Pan program, oral interviews with former students, teachers and administrators, and statistics that support the tenets behind the need to establish a bilingual program. We are afforded the opportunity to see the report cards that were used, images of the daily schedules, sample letters to parents, evaluations submitted to the Ford Foundation and so much more.

The Coral Way Bilingual Program offers something for everyone. For the English-speaking parents who took the risk to trust what the educators promised, this book reassures them that they gave their children a lifelong gift. For the students themselves, both English and Spanish speakers, who participated in the program, the book will help them to relive the days when without knowing what was being done, they were acquiring a new language and culture that would forever enrich their lives. For the academic, the researcher, Dr Coady dedicates a chapter to describing the research design, the data and the findings. For those of us who worked at Coral Way Elementary at one time or another, we can continue to take pride in knowing that we were part of a school whose contributions to education resonate across the world.

The education community, and more specifically the bilingual community, applaud Dr Coady for this important publication. It sheds light on the beginnings of a movement that today continues to be misunderstood and undervalued. In studying and learning about the success of the first two-way immersion program in a public school, we can continue to forge the future based on proven experiences and research.

Lourdes Rovira
Miami, FL

Overview

This book is about Coral Way Elementary school and the events that took place between 1961–1968, seven years that changed the landscape of education in the United States and arguably around the world. These six years allow readers to experience the social, political and educational context in which the Coral Way bilingual program was conceptualized (1961–1963), how the early two-way immersion model of bilingual education in the United States was implemented and subsequently changed (1963–1968) and the outcomes of the Coral Way 'experiment' based on student achievement data and interview data from the program's participants. For readers' reference, I build the context of the program based on political events that took place in Cuba and the United States between 1960 and 1962, and describe the Cuban refugee context and Operation Pedro Pan, which brought more than 14,000 unaccompanied youth to the United States by late 1962 (Conde, 1999). I also discuss the larger field and context of bilingual education in the United States, noting that although Coral Way is believed to be the first two-way immersion bilingual education program in the United States, bilingual education programs were not uncommon in the United States and were especially prevalent for German and Dutch speakers up until World War II (Baker & Wright, 2017; Ovando, 2003).

Based in its historical context and the model of bilingual education it followed, Coral Way is undoubtedly a legacy in the field of bilingual education, and its teachers and leaders its pioneers. Prior to this volume, we have had little knowledge about what happened during the formative years of the program's development and, more importantly, what decisions were made that led to this particular model. Despite our limited knowledge, books on bilingual education, dual-language education and two-way immersion programs have referenced Coral Way to varying degrees. For instance, some scholars have referenced Coral Way in single lines (Bearse & de Jong, 2008; Boyle *et al.*, 2015), short verses (Andersson, 1971; Berney & Eisenberg, 1968; Castellanos & Leggio, 1983; Craig, 1995; García & Otheguy, 1985; Hakuta, 1986; Jacobson, 1974; Lyons, 1990; Ovando, 2003) or, rarely, as a complete chapter (Mackey & Beebe, 1977; Pellerano *et al.*, 1998). A more recent study of language ideologies and uses in Coral Way as a K-8 center was conducted by MacKinney (2016), with some limited treatment of its sociohistorical roots. However, none has thoroughly examined the Coral Way program itself, nor the nature of the experiment aimed at building bilingualism and biliteracy among both native Spanish- and native English-speaking children. The Coral Way bilingual program[1] contributes to the history of bilingual education in the United States and offers an extensive review of the early days of the first known two-way immersion program in the United States.

Readers of this book will find data derived from more than 900 pages from the school and the Ford Foundation archives; oral histories and interviews conducted with educators and students affiliated with Coral Way; newspaper articles and journal articles. Material artifacts, school photographs and imagery have also been examined, as well as any literature mentioning or describing Coral Way in academic textbooks, journals, theses and periodicals. Quantitative data on the achievement of students who participated in the Coral Way experiment between 1963 and 1966, although sparse, are also included for readers to examine. But perhaps most telling are the voices of the teachers and students, some of whom recall their conversations with their parents, now deceased, about their education, and who retrieve their memories of the days at Coral Way while acknowledging, 'I don't know if I'm coloring [my memories] with nostalgia, but everybody seemed pretty happy, in spite of... the trauma of having to leave Cuba and what was happening in Cuba at the time'.[2] We must remember that memories are shaped and reshaped over time, and although 50 years have passed for many of those who participated in the experiment, Orestes Gonzalez's earlier quote is a resounding and confirming sentiment across many of the students.

I provide additional context for the current Coral Way K-8 Center in both the Prologue and Epilogue of this book, and in the Epilogue I connect Coral Way Elementary (the experimental bilingual program) to the Coral Way K-8 Center today. In Chapters 1–6, I offer readers the opportunity to examine the bilingual education program and experiment between 1961 and 1966. Chapter 1 describes the context and influx of Cubans to the Miami area between 1960 and 1962 and into 1963, when the bilingual education experiment began. Readers will note that particularly in education, context plays an essential role in how leaders build teams of support and how teachers and aides conceptualize their work with students. Teachers also negotiate the context of education as they implement instructional practices and navigate educational programs and policies (Darling-Hammond, 2017), particularly with students learning a second language (Coady *et al.*, 2016). This is because language, is an integral part of our individual and social identities and of the language policies that we enact.

Chapter 2 discusses the bilingual education program model, which some readers might know as a two-way immersion or a 50:50 model of bilingual education. In today's terminology, this model of bilingual education is increasingly referred to simply as 'dual language'. However, readers should caution that dual language as a term did not exist in the 1960s, and today the term 'dual language' eclipses some important variations across programs when it is used. In the 1960s, the Coral Way program was referred to simply as the 'bilingual school'. In this book, I retain the original terminology used by the early founders of the program when I cite their stories and data from the archives, but I refer to the program model as two-way immersion in the book's Epilogue in order to keep with current terminology. However, labels do matter and I am sensitive to the variation in terminology used by scholars, teachers and politicians, and how this affects public perception of bilingualism and bilingual education.

The Coral Way bilingual program itself went through several important student and teacher configurations over the first few years of its implementation. It was, after all, an experiment and was described this way by its early visionaries. I describe the challenges that teachers faced in determining which students were considered native Spanish and native English speakers. Chapter 2 also includes images from student report cards, which demonstrate the development of the model between 1962 and 1963 and how serious the educators were in building a second language for both English- and Spanish-speaking students.

Chapter 3 describes teacher education and how Cuban aides, who were primarily highly educated, former teachers in Cuba, were trained to become teachers who taught Spanish- and English-speaking children through the medium of Spanish. This chapter notes the emphasis on teacher professional development during the summer months of 1962 and 1963 and work that was funded by the Ford Foundation. The summer professional development emphasized the need for teachers to conceptualize instruction in two languages and to collaborate in order to design and implement a new curriculum.

Chapter 4 narrows in on the innovation and development of the *Miami Linguistic Readers* and literacy development for bilingual children, the use of the audiolingual teaching method and educational curriculum in general. The Miami Linguistic Readers, like Coral Way itself, was considered a groundbreaking curriculum, composed of teaching materials, student books, 'big books' and workbooks for children learning English as a second language. The curriculum and materials were later used and distributed nationally, and readers can find examples of the books in mainstream online storefronts. I provide some visual examples of the readers in this book as well.

Chapter 5 attempts to answer the question that readers, teachers and scholars of bilingual education frequently ask: Did the experiment work? And if so, how? Using both qualitative data derived from documents and material artifacts and oral histories and interviews, in addition to student achievement data from limited sources, readers are presented with answers to these questions. The answers are not restricted, however, to data on student learning, or even bilingual development assessed using oral and written assessments. The answers lie in the voices of the students who graduated from Coral Way, their life experiences and the extended networks that they built and maintain to this day. Answers also derive from parents and teachers of Coral Way. Notably, not every child enjoyed the Coral Way bilingual program, and as we continue to conduct oral histories with graduates of the first class, this point is elucidated.

Chapter 6 discusses the building of a bilingual network. I use data and information from the Coral Way archives on visitors to the school, and I refer to new and emerging bilingual education programs that appeared somewhat simultaneous to and immediately after the establishment of Coral Way. Finally, I conclude this book with an Epilogue and, like the Prologue, provide readers with connections to bilingual education policies in the current context. As previously noted, I connect the Coral Way bilingual program to today's two-way immersion programs, referred to frequently as 'dual language'. Ultimately, I argue that scholars and educators in the field of bilingual education face the daunting yet essential task of making known the multilingual landscape of the United States, the language-as-resource paradigm in education (Ruiz, 1984) and our collective work as 'movement intellectuals' (Machado-Casas *et al.*, 2015: 33). Our future is rooted in our past. To paraphrase social historian David McCullough (1992), how can we know who we are and where we are going unless we know where we are from, the courage shown and the price paid to get here?

Notes

(1) Coral Way was a monolingual (English medium) neighborhood elementary school from 1936 until 1962. In 1963, it began a two-way program with first-grade students and became a fully bilingual (two-way immersion) school by 1967–1968. It remains a fully bilingual school today.

(2) Gonzalez, O. (2008, March 26) Interview by R. Ruiz [audio file]. Coral Way Elementary. University of Florida Digital Collections. See https://ufdc.ufl.edu/AA00065599/00001.

References

Andersson, T. (1971) Bilingual Education: The American Experience. Paper presented at the Ontario Institute for Studies in Education Conference. Toronto, Canada.

Baker, C. and Wright, W.E. (2017) *Foundations of Bilingual Education and Bilingualism* (6th edn). Bristol: Multilingual Matters.

Bearse, C. and de Jong, E.J. (2008) Cultural and linguistic investment: Adolescents in a secondary two-way immersion program. *Equity & Excellence in Education* 41 (3), 325–340.

Berney, T.D. and Eisenberg, A. (1968) *Doble Research Supplement. Digest of Bilingual Education*. Washington, DC: ERIC.

Boyle, A., August, D., Tabaku, L., Cole, S. and Simpson-Baird, A. (2015) *Dual Language Education Programs: Current State Policies and Practices*. Washington, DC: American Institutes for Research.

Castellanos, D. and Leggio, P. (1983) *The Best of Two Worlds: Bilingual-Bicultural Education in the US*. Trenton, NJ: NJ State Department of Education.

Coady, M., Harper, C. and de Jong, E. (2016) Aiming for equity: Preparing mainstream teachers for inclusion or inclusive classrooms? *TESOL Quarterly* 50 (2), 340–368. doi: 10.1002/tesq.223

Conde, Y.M. (1999) *Operation Pedro Pan: The Untold Exodus of 14,048 Cuban Children*. New York: Routledge.

Craig, B.A. (1995) Two-Way Foreign Language Immersion Programs: A Handbook for Parents and Teachers. ERIC document ED384239.

Darling-Hammond, L. (2017) Current issues in teacher education: An interview with Dr. Linda Darling-Hammond. *The Teacher Educator* 52 (2), 75–83.

García, O. and Otheguy, R. (1985) The masters of survival send their children to school: Bilingual education in the ethnic schools of Miami. *The Bilingual Review/La Revista Bilingüe* 12, 3–19.

Hakuta, K. (1986) *The Mirror of Language: The Debate on Bilingualism*. New York: Basic.

Jacobson, K. (1974) Bilingual/bicultural education: Why? for whom? what? how? *Minnesota Language Review* 3 (2), 74–84.

Lyons, J.J. (1990) The past and future directions of federal bilingual-education policy. *The Annals of the American Academy of Political and Social Science* 508, 66–80.

Machado-Casas, M., Flores, B.B. and Murillo, Jr, E. (2015) Reframing: We are not public intellectuals; we are movement intellectuals. In C. Gerstl-Pepin and C. Reyes (eds) *Reimagining the Public Intellectual in Education* (pp. 31–37). New York: Peter Lange.

Mackey, W.F. and Beebe, V.N. (1977) *Bilingual Schools for a Bicultural Community: Miami's Adaptation to the Cuban Refugees*. Rowley, MA: Newbury House Publishers.

MacKinney, E. (2016) Language ideologies and bilingual realities: The case of Coral Way. In N.H. Hornberger (ed.) *Honoring Richard Ruiz and His Work on Language Planning and Bilingual Education* (pp. 301–315). Bristol: Multilingual Matters.

McCullough, D. (1992) *Brave Companions: Portraits in History*. New York: Simon & Schuster.

Ovando, C.J. (2003) Bilingual education in the United States: Historical development and current issues. *Bilingual Research Journal* 27 (1), 1–25.

Pellerano, C., Fradd, S.H. and Rovira, L. (1998) Coral Way Elementary School: A success story in bilingualism and biliteracy. *Discover*, 3. National Clearinghouse for Bilingual Education, Washington, DC.

Ruiz, R. (1984) Orientations in language planning. *NABE Journal* 7 (2), 15–34.

Prologue

Fall 2018

I arrive at Coral Way at 8:50am. A crossing guard dressed in a green reflective vest vigorously waves on a yellow school bus. Young children cross the street holding their mother's hand and hug goodbye before skipping through the front entrance of the school. It's an idyllic American school scene – the morning dew, the hug, the school gate – repeated a million times each school day across the United States. Except this scene takes place in front of the earliest bilingual 'two-way immersion' (TWI) program in the United States.[1,2]

Turning left onto Southwest 13th Avenue is a chain-link fence with 'Faculty' marked on the side of the school. The gate is open, and although there are about 30 parking spaces, only a handful of cars are parked. I maneuver the neon blue Mini Cooper rental just under the shade of an oak tree, which is big enough to cast shadows that will keep the car cool throughout the day. It's already hot on this October morning, but the Miami humidity has yet to set in, thickening the air until white puffs of clouds converge into ominous black afternoon storms. This season, south Florida has been left unscathed by hurricanes. I hope to stay at the school until 12 or 1pm if I am lucky. But I know that Susana Córdoba Martín, the lead bilingual teacher who organized my visit, will be busy. Teachers are always busy, wizards and wizardesses of the multitask.

Susana informed me via email that today is 'Meet the Author' day for the second-grade students. I had hoped to meet the interim principal today, too, but three prior emails and phone calls hadn't been successful. I finally got in touch with Susana through several colleagues who were education professors and linguists in Miami, some already retired from long careers in bilingual education. Susana immediately messaged me back to arrange my time at the school. I told her I was interested in the school's important history and its contributions. I wanted to learn more.

1

Visitors are welcome here, and Coral Way has had plenty of national and international visitors since 1963.

Entering the doorway, I find a portable black desk with a computer and a security guard named Pablo standing behind it. He greets me with a smile. The desk is a mini table on wheels, and Pablo angles it slightly as I approach, caddy corner to a green metal door across the hallway, indicating the school's main office. The light from the Coral Way entrance is at my back, and behind Pablo's shoulder is the courtyard fountain of Coral Way, an icon that shows up repeatedly in photographs and archives that portray the history of the school. The building itself is historic, constructed in 1936, a mixture of Spanish and art deco designs (Pellerano *et al.*, 1998), with round archways and corbels under terracotta tiled roofs and stucco exterior walls. This could easily be Havana or Seville with open courtyards under the shade of palms.

This fitting architecture has welcomed Cuban and other immigrant children to the school for more than five decades. Generations of families have attended Coral Way, and it has become almost commonplace for me to hear stories about parents who attended and subsequently insisted on sending their kids to this neighborhood school. Like any program, not all children enjoyed Coral Way, and not all parents understood what its aims were on 3 September 1963, when it opened its doors as the first TWI bilingual education program.

The term 'two-way immersion' did not exist in the 1960s, and as noted in the Overview of this book, nor did current terminology such as 'dual language' or even 'one-way immersion'. Despite the different terminologies used between the 1960s and today, which describe a variety of language learning program types and models, bilingual education has existed from before the founding of the United States. For instance, Feinberg (2002) reports the opening of a German school as early as 1734 and the significant growth in German language schools across 15 states over the subsequent century. Spanish was used as a medium of instruction in schools in the early 20th century in the states of Arizona, New Mexico and Texas, and French and English were authorized for instructional purposes in Louisiana (Baker & Wright, 2017; Feinberg, 2002; Ovando, 2003; Wright, 2019).

Baker and Wright (2017: 172) remind us that there are two risks associated with the 'illusion' of bilingual education as a modern movement. First is the danger of believing that bilingual education has only existed in recent times, thereby neglecting the long history of bilingual education in the United States. They noted that bilingualism and bilingual education have existed in a variety of forms for more than 5000 years. Second, scholars run the risk of separating the current movement and growth in bilingual education programs in the United States from their sociopolitical context. Examining the origins of the Coral Way bilingual program, the sociopolitical context in which the program began and the inspiration for the program based on other programs around the world might address those noted risks. In the Epilogue of this book, I return to the current context of Coral Way and the growth of TWI programs today as a way to connect the past with current bilingual movements.

Also, as will become clearer throughout this book, language ideologies and bilingual education are deeply intertwined. MacKinney defines the complexity of language ideologies as

> Sets of beliefs, feelings and conceptions about language that form a mediating link between social structures and language practices. They are not only about language; rather they envision and enact links of language to group and personal identity... [they are] constructed through one's own experiences and in the interests of a particular social or cultural group.... [and] are often unnoticed and taken for granted. (MacKinney, 2016: 301–302)

MacKinney (2016: 302) continues that 'schools provide a crucial context in which to explore the intersection of language ideologies and language policies'. Coral Way is one example of the intersection of language beliefs or ideologies and educational programs. In another example in the United States, languages spoken by indigenous people, estimated between 250 and 1000 at the time of European colonization of the North American continent in the 15th century, were considered savage and uncivilized (Adams, 1995). Ideologies toward indigenous people led to repressive language policies and linguistic and cultural genocide (Ovando, 2003; Warhol, 2011). Indigenous-speaking children were forced into boarding schools, referred to as indigenous residential schools, and were required to speak English only (Adams, 1995), resulting in extreme consequences on children's 'psychological and cultural being' (Adams, 1995: 336).

In contrast to the assimilationist language policies that characterize indigenous schools (Warhol, 2011), when Coral Way opened its doors to children who came from different language and cultural backgrounds – American English and Cuban Spanish – many did not know that the school was opening its doors to a novel type of bilingual education program. In the Coral Way TWI program, both English-speaking and Spanish-speaking children would listen, speak, read and write in two languages, with the aim of building fully bilingual and biliterate students from different language backgrounds. The establishment of the Coral Way bilingual program was predicated on the temporary stay of Cuban children and families, following Castro's rise to power in the late 1950s. In addition, there appeared to be social acceptance of well-educated and light-skinned Cubans who sought refuge from communism (Stepick & Stepick, 2009). Hence, there was a sense of cultural and linguistic accommodation rather than assimilation, and the commitment of teachers at Coral Way, who took very seriously the charge of biliteracy. With respect to bilingualism, the main mission of the school from its inception has been

> two-fold; to assist English speaking pupils to speak, read and write both in English and Spanish; and to assist the Spanish speaking pupils to speak, read and write in both languages. (Richardson, 1964: 3)

The stories of teachers, students, parents and administrators of the school are speckled throughout this book as a way of illuminating the story of Coral Way, its concepts, processes, challenges and successes, which pioneered a new generation of educational programs in the United States and, indeed, worldwide.

Why is the History of Coral Way Important?

Analyzing data for this book, I encountered various histories and stories that lay claim to Coral Way being either the first bilingual education program in the United States, the first publicly funded program or the earliest TWI program. Coral Way was not the first bilingual education program in the United States, as previously noted, but scholars of bilingual education acknowledge that Coral Way Elementary was among the first, if not the first, bilingual education program that included both language minoritized and English-speaking children in the same program with the stated goal of developing bilingualism and biliteracy for both groups (Baker & Wright, 2017; Mackey & Beebe, 1977; Ovando, 2003; Wright, 2019).

Based on my analysis of archival data, Coral Way appears to have been the earliest TWI bilingual education program in the United States, but the degree to which its funding derived entirely from private sources (essentially the Ford Foundation) or public federal and local sources, such as from the federal Cuban Refugee Program (Mitchell, 1962), is less clear. MacKinney's (2016: 304) study of language policies and practices at Coral Way described the school as 'the oldest Spanish–English public bilingual program' in the United States. Despite these different views of its status, what makes Coral Way unique is how it aimed to provide bilingual education in English and Spanish to two distinct groups of children: English and Spanish speaking. As I note in Chapter 2, however, those distinctions were neither clear to teachers nor accurate. I also found in my investigation that Coral Way was not the first program of its type worldwide. As I detail in Chapter 1, data describe Dr Pauline Rojas's international travel and anecdotes which indicate that she took inspiration for Coral Way from a school she visited while examining bilingual education programs abroad.

The wider context in which Coral Way was established, however, adds to the important question of how bilingual education programs can be established in the current sociopolitical climate, which in Florida, for example, is highly restrictive in terms of both native language use and maintenance in school. The history of Coral Way does provide insight into the longitudinal prospect of TWI programs, and the intersection of context and program development. In essence, the sociopolitical context of Cuban refugees who were considered temporary sojourners in the United States contributed to a favorable climate for the Coral Way program. Simultaneously, across the United States there were other movements for language rights in the southwest and northeast that sought linguistic rights for bilinguals and non-English speakers (Escamilla, 2018; Peterson, 2017).

Yet, among scholars and educators of bilingual education, Coral Way is considered a well-known legacy. Surprisingly, beyond a fleeting paragraph in an educational textbook or a line in an academic journal, little is known about the school itself, the social experiment conducted or the outcomes of those students who participated. Interestingly, even students who graduated from Coral Way, then quite young, fail to fully understand the impact of the program in which they participated. How did this legacy – so important to education in the United States – become so overlooked? And how did it become oft-referenced as a short-lived program from the 1960s in educational books and references? The school still operates successfully today.[3]

I am ruminating over these questions when I am brought back to reality by Pablo, who asks for my ID, a 21st-century security precaution to enter a school and to be in the presence of children. As I hand him my Florida driver's license, he tells me that he has worked at the school for 27 years and still lives across the street from the school. A dutiful and proud father, all of his children attended the school. Pablo had been expecting my arrival and already knew the purpose of my visit: to conduct research on Coral Way's history. As if on cue, Pablo spends several minutes recounting his tenure at Coral Way. 'Entonces, has visto muchos cambios durante esos años?' ['So, you have seen many changes over those years?'] I ask him. 'Sí, claro' ['Yes, of course'], he replies gleefully and somewhat reservedly. He inserts my driver's license into the background check machine while speaking into a walkie-talkie. 'Suzy, la señora Coady está aquí' ['Suzy, Mrs. Coady is here']. 'Un minuto' ['One minute'], I hear Susana respond. Ten seconds later, the machine prints a visitor's badge, and Pablo unpeels the back of the label for me to stick on my shirt. 'I hope you enjoy your visit', he comments just as Susana walks up to the entrance, walkie-talkie in hand. She's moving quickly, responding simultaneously to announcements, teacher requests and a variety of individual student logistics.

Susana and I walk through the art deco courtyard. Four playfully painted park benches surround the famous Coral Way fountain, which catches me off guard. Pictures portray the fountain as a symmetrical icon, but it is built off-center with the apex to my right side. Although the tiles are no longer white, as depicted in earlier photos, the Spanish style is retained. Few tiles are missing and it is in remarkably good shape. Susana tells me about the various changes it has undergone over the years and that the apex was only added in the past decade.

Her walkie-talkie buzzes. The author and his team for the second-grade reading event have arrived early and are waiting at the middle school entrance. There are two entrances to Coral Way, Susana explains, alternating between Spanish and English. 'We'll have to walk down there and get them settled. Sorry', she remarks. 'No, no te preocupes', I reply. 'I'm here to learn from you, about the school. Don't worry about me'. We're walking fast, so I take mental notes about the languages I hear, the multicultural cutout figures that are decorated in traditional costumes from various Latin American countries and displayed on a hallway bulletin board. The caption over the cutouts reads, Todos Unidos Celebramos La Hispanidad – In Unity We Celebrate Hispanic Heritage. Two of the figures have actual student pictures for faces, representing the diversity of students studying in these classrooms.

Susana's long, thick hair is cut straight across her back. It would be difficult to guess that she has worked at Coral Way for 22 years, beginning in 1996 as an English teacher during the summer months, then pregnant with her second son. She starts to describe the importance of bilingualism to the school, her own bilingual journey and that of her sons', but the walkie-talkie is impatient, and there's a lot of activity for a Friday morning.

Toño Malpica, the author of the children's book, whose name I find fun to replay in my mind, and his team are setting up the author's books

Image P.1 Coral Way fountain, 2018. *Source*: Maria Coady

and microphone in the middle school cafeteria. The middle school was constructed when the school expanded to Grades 7 and 8 in 2004. This, then, is the school's new cafeteria.

Waiting for the second-grade classes to arrive, Toño, short for Antonio, plans how and when he will sign the books as a gift to each of the students. The team, which now includes Susana, calculates that it will take 15 minutes to sign all of the books if Toño writes quickly. They don't want to squander any of the allocated 45 minutes with the children for the book-signing task, so it is decided, just as the children are ushered into the cafeteria, that Toño will sign them after the students leave.

This moment is characteristic of the inner-workings and culture of Coral Way. Time is precious, and minutes are jewels of opportunity through which children build bilingualism and biliteracy. Malpica's (2017) book is called *Esa Mañana*, not exactly a bilingual book, Susana corrects, but a book written in Spanish. Susana read the book before scheduling the author and determined it was most appropriate for second-grade students this year. But original authors come frequently to the school to share their work, and Coral Way, two stones' throw from downtown Miami, benefits from access to a bilingual–biliterate community.

Susana continues to explain the school's primary mission of biliteracy development and its extended history with Spanish literature and authentic authors. Her own office, the resource room for the Spanish bilingual teachers, is replete with books, posters, inspirations, dichos (sayings), and flyers from the community's annual Festival de Lectura – Reading Festival – in Miami, which happens to be taking place this week. Susana points out a book written by her cousin Eduardo Otero, an accomplished medical doctor who attended Coral Way and wanted to instill Spanish literacy in his own children by authoring *El Alfabeto Cubano* (Otero, 2009). Like Otero, other graduates of Coral Way have gone on to become immensely successful adults in a wide variety of careers. Between Cuban coffee, literature, architecture and books, it is evident that Coral Way is no typical school.

Toño Malpica's first question to the 33 seated-but-fidgeting second graders is, '¿de dónde son sus padres?' Where are your parents from? The students and their two teachers – the Spanish and English teachers – sit on dark green cafeteria tables turned into benches. 'Tell me with a show of hands', he continues in Spanish. Toño begins to rattle off the names of Spanish-speaking countries: México, one hand goes up; Venezuela, two hands; Argentina, five hands; Cuba, eight more; Ecuador, one; Colombia, two; Puerto Rico, three hands; and la República Dominicana, two hands are raised high. He pauses before continuing, 'Nicaragua', four hands jolt upward; Costa Rica, one; '¿y qué más?'. The students shout 'Honduras' as they wiggle around on the benches. Two hands. 'Síííí', Toño encourages, 'Hondureños, claro'. The children shout, 'Guatemala' and two more hands rise. The students state, 'y los Estados Unidos' – the United States, and the final few hands dart up. In the 55 years of Coral Way as a TWI program, this has become a decidedly bilingual, biliterate and multicultural, international school. How it got this way – and how it perseveres – is an extraordinary story.

To unravel the story of Coral Way and its contribution to bilingual education, easily characterized as a social experiment in education, it is necessary to understand the context in which the school began. I am neither an historian nor an expert in US political relations. I am a bilingual educator who studies bi- and multilingual language development in schools and bilingual education programs worldwide. In my dissertation work, I investigated one-way immersion in Irish Gaeilge in the Republic of Ireland (Coady, 2001). To the uninitiated general American public, building literacy in students' first languages, such as Spanish, is frequently and inaccurately portrayed as a 'waste of time', because it takes time away from students learning English. This is a flawed argument of exactly why *not* to support and grow bilingual education programs. But this is precisely why scholars conduct research and why good research on bilingual education is essential: We know that high levels of native language literacy build high levels of literacy in English. The time-on-task argument is, in fact, a weak one when it comes to bilingual students and language development (MacSwan *et al.*, 2017). Bilingual education is counter-intuitive: more first language development actually fosters the second language.

Many noteworthy scholars have written about the effectiveness of bilingual education, studied its various components and continue to conduct meta-analyses and even meta-analysis of the meta-analyses (McField & McField, 2014). Their work has unequivocally shown over the past 40 years that bilingual education is highly effective in supporting language and literacy development for bilingual children, more so than an intensive English-only approach. Early research on bilingual education has even been funded by the US Department of Education (Thomas & Collier, 1997), which should raise eyebrows as to why there aren't more bilingual education programs in the United States, a question I hope that readers will keep in mind as they read this historical account of Coral Way, its mission and, ultimately, its student learning outcomes.

Contributions of Dr Richard Ruiz

When I began to read the 1960s archives on Coral Way, which were collected by Dr Richard Ruiz and Bess de Farber from the University of Arizona in 2007 and 2008, I was simultaneously transported back 50 years and standing in the present time. Many of the issues and challenges that early bilingual educators and scholars faced between 1961 and 1968 are the same – or at least very similar – to those that bilingual educators face today: the desire for high-quality bilingual curriculum and materials; targeted, effective teacher education; and innovative, research-based teaching methods. This statement is no surprise to educators who lament the proverbial 'swinging of the pendulum' in educational policies and practices. New movements in, others out. New policies in, others out. What is surprising, however, is that Coral Way Elementary, now the Coral Way K-8 Center, has weathered many changes in educational policies and practices, and continues today as an exemplary program in and model of bilingual education. Coral Way's short story is that children enter the school with varying degrees of one or two languages but leave the school highly bilingual and biliterate. They outperform peers, in general, in monolingual English-only programs. That is one reason why today there are more than 2000 dual-language, TWI programs in the United States and growing (Boyle *et al.*, 2015; Wilson, 2011).

Richard Ruiz was a pioneer in the field of bilingual education. To my own regret, I never met Richard personally, but my mentors in bilingual education – Drs Kathy Escamilla and María Fránquiz – were his peers. Along with other important scholars and students of Richard's, they paid great tribute to Richard's life and work in 2016, a year after his sudden passing, in a special issue of the *Bilingual Research Journal*. Surprisingly, his work on Coral Way was not known, had not been documented, nor had it emerged in any scholarly publications at the time of his death. Even today, I am not sure why.

Over the years, I have read and referenced Richard's work many times in my own work. Perhaps his most well-known contribution to language planning and bilingualism was his framework and 1984 article, 'Orientations in Language Planning', which describes three orientations in conceptualizing language: as a problem, as a right and as a resource.[4] These are not mutually exclusive to each other, and scholars today identify these orientations simultaneously in classrooms and in the public sphere. Indeed, the various co-existing orientations remind us that language use and language ideologies are complex acts, and people make decisions about language use and language development based more on emotion and ideology than on research about what works. In his article, Richard wrote:

> [o]rientations are related to *language attitudes* in that they constitute the framework in which attitudes are formed: they help to delimit the range of acceptable attitudes toward language, and to make certain attitudes legitimate. In short, orientations determine what is thinkable about language in society. (Ruiz, 1984: 16) [emphasis retained]

Individuals can hold one view of language policies for themselves and their children, yet at the same time cling to another at a community or societal level. For instance, parents can want their children to become bilingual or to attain some level of language ability in order to get ahead in school and in society – to build social capital – yet they may overtly support monolingual, English-only policies for the broader community or society. As I discuss in the Epilogue of this book, this multifaceted position regarding bilingualism has important present-day effects on the growth of TWI programs in the United States.

The general public's view of language unfortunately persists in positioning languages other than English in the United States as problems, as evidenced in Florida's official English policy passed by the state legislature in 1988, 25 years after Coral Way was established as a two-way bilingual education program. An unstated mission of English-only in Florida and other assimilationist educational and social policies aim to eradicate language minoritized students' native languages (if they are non-native English speakers), at least until they have allegedly mastered English, upon which they can return to their native languages and relearn them. Yet, such policies are swiftly reversed for native English speakers who are provided with a steady supply of Spanish, French or other 50-minute daily foreign language classes in middle and high school so that students can gain social capital by parents who want their teens to get ahead, enter college and demonstrate some knowledge of an additional language, albeit to embarrassingly low levels of language ability.

In the midst of the language-as-problem orientation is the reality that Florida, like so many US states, is highly *multilingual*. More than 200 languages are spoken in Florida's schools, and we have about 300,000 identified learners of English across Florida's 67 school districts (Florida Department of Education, 2018). Yet, unfortunately, proportionately few students are provided with instruction in the home language, which would benefit both the students and the state, academically, socially, cognitively and economically (Coady, 2019; Gándara, 2015). If the reader does not believe the research, I invite you to read the words of former students of Coral Way such as Diana Morales, Leticia Lopez, Catherina Poerschke and Orestes Gonzalez, who attribute their professional success directly to their high levels of bilingual ability developed at Coral Way. I can't help but wonder: when did we become ashamed to acknowledge our own multilingual reality?

Arguments for one-language, one-state policies are lost on countries worldwide. Consider any European country, or any country in the world for that matter. No country has a populace that uses one language exclusively. At the individual level, however, we recognize the importance of proficiency in more than one language. How many times has the reader heard, 'if only my [grand]parents had insisted that we use the [X] language at home'?

In one of the 12 oral history recordings that Richard conducted, he introduces himself to former Coral Way teachers and staff as a professor of bilingual education and language planning. Richard's contribution to our field cannot be underestimated, and I appreciated his humility in his own introduction to the staff at Coral Way. I do wish I had known Richard personally, because in the process of learning the story of Coral Way and listening to the oral histories he conducted, I also listened to him. I heard his voice. I heard how Richard approached participants in the project, the care with which he listened, Richard's desire to keep the project going after the initial oral histories were conducted, and his genuine desire to tell the school's story. I also heard Richard chuckle, start and stop a recording after not following the prescribed oral history protocol, pause in amazement at some of the early stories of the school and the outcomes of its students, and express his hope to build an archive of this material at the Historical Museum of Southern Florida.

Richard's work reflected how languages are rooted in communities. Several of the questions that Richard asked the participants in the oral histories between 2007 and 2008 specifically aimed at unearthing the relationship the students' use of language at school and its relationship to the home and community. In 1997, Richard wrote:

A central and early tenet of bilingual education advocates was that inclusion of the child's language and culture in the curriculum would lead to greater school achievement... More recently, this discussion has turned from a consideration of merely cognitive and academic consequences of mother tongue instruction and bilingualism to their sociolinguistic and political consequences as well. This goes beyond suggestions that being bilingual can be of some academic or commercial advantage: it entails a general reordering of prevailing societal patterns of stratification. In other words, native language instruction can be an important factor in ethnic communities shedding their minority status by sharing power with the dominant group. (Ruiz, 1997: 319)

Thus, Richard aimed to examine the relationship between native language instruction in school, social patterns and the relationship between ethnic communities and dominant group(s). From the 2007 and 2008 audio recordings, it seemed clear that Richard wanted to ensure that people knew how the first TWI bilingual education program began and how it affected not only its students, teachers, principals and aides, but also the families, the surrounding community and the United States. He described Coral Way to his students at the University of Arizona, and inspired a new generation of scholars to carefully examine language policies and bilingual education (MacKinney, 2016). In an introductory article as editor of the *Bilingual Research Journal*, Ruiz wrote:

[w]e have to acknowledge that the scholar's work is political, perhaps in the most fundamental sense. What we do can determine how the public dialogue about bilingualism and bilingual education is fashioned – the terms it uses, its contours... we must keep in mind the power that can accrue to a cause that uses research to find out what is true, nor merely what is convenient, about the world. (Ruiz, 1995, cited in Fránquiz *et al.*, 2016: 169)

This work, then, is dedicated to Richard's vision and to scholars and educators who must take the work we do and make it accessible, readable and understandable to the public. In a recent graduate course I held on bilingual education, a master's degree student, who had digested a large amount of research on the effectiveness of bilingual education, turned and asked me, 'Dr. Coady, this work is so difficult to read but important. Why can't researchers write it so that people like teachers can understand it?'.

To emphasize Richard's earlier point, the scholar's work is political. We do shape public dialogue about bilingualism and bilingual education, yet we do a poor job of informing the prepared teacher, the politician and general public about our findings. Contrary to those who initially claim that more English leads to faster and more effective English language development – the 'time-on-task' argument – we know that high levels of native language development lead to higher achievement, richer intercultural dialogue, deeper human understanding and more equitable communities, and – if this is our benchmark – to more English, as well. This is what Coral Way proves, and this is why this book is so important. I take it as my task to make this work understandable to readers who may not know about bilingual education or who might not understand why and how bilingual education works.

In 2007 and 2008, Richard worked with Coral Way graduate Bess de Farber. Bess was recruited to serve as the University of Arizona Libraries' first grants manager in 2005, an experimental position. She learned of Richard's research in bilingual education and emailed him on a whim to ask if he was interested in chatting about her 1960s experiences at Coral Way Elementary. Richard replied within minutes and asked to meet with Bess. Richard shared that Coral Way was the first federally funded bilingual school in the country, and that Bess's experiences did not match up with what was known in the scholarly community about the school. Until meeting Richard, she had no previous knowledge about the impact of those first six years on the field of bilingual education. They began the process of locating other graduates from the first classes of Coral Way. The following year, Bess and Richard traveled from Arizona to Miami and conducted the first oral histories of the earlier project. Bess also donated many of her personal school items from Coral Way to the archives at the University of Arizona. In 2019–20 the University of Florida acquired the UA archives and continues to build the collection at the University of Florida. In 2008, Bess was recruited for a similar position as grants manager at the University of Florida Libraries, where Richard had encouraged her to reach out to me to continue the project, and possibly to host a Coral Way reunion of those who had contributed their oral histories to the digital archive, but I didn't meet Bess until 2017, nearly two years after Richard passed away. In 2019, the University of Arizona gifted the digital and material Coral Way collections to the Univeristy of Florida (UF). The entire collection is at UF, with new oral histories and materials.

Conclusion

I believe that Richard did have an ulterior motive beyond documenting the early days of Coral Way, how it was conceptualized and implemented, and the stories of the people who committed themselves and their waking hours to the children in the school and their language and literacy development. I surmise that Richard intended for us to understand the past in order for us to progress in the future. We cannot know where we are going, unless we know from where we come. Nadia Granados, a former student of Richard's writes:

> You reminded us to never forget our history and that there is no progress without committed individuals who have a devoted interest in human rights and promoting change. It is through your work that we better understand how educators and policy makers must bring issues of language learning to the forefront and to consider the relationship between language and power in society. (Granados, 2016: 369)

The sankofa is a fitting image to capture TWI bilingual education programs in the United States today and the role of Coral Way Elementary School. The sankofa is a graceful, long neck bird, whose eyes and beak are turned 180 degrees backward, while its feet are firmly rooted forward, in the direction of the future. The bird holds a precious egg in its beak, the egg itself symbolic of new beginnings and life. The bird rests graciously in the present moment, a twinkle of time that reflects the entirety of its past while acknowledging the imminence of the future. Coral Way embodies the origin of the first TWI program and, like the symbolic bird, is rooted in the present with a foothold into the future.

This project is dedicated to Richard, to Bess and to the visionaries and leaders of the Coral Way experiment.

Image P.2 Richard Ruiz. *Source*: University of Arizona permission granted from Marie Ruiz. https://www.coe.arizona.edu/richardruizremembrance

Notes

(1) To my knowledge and from my research and to underscore the point in the Overview of this book, none of the early founders referred to the program as dual language, two-way or immersion. The program was referred to as 'the bilingual program' or 'the bilingual school'. Hornberger (1991) differentiates *model* of bilingual education from *program types*. García (2009: 114) notes that there is 'no tight representation of systems, and the same model may have very different features depending on how the many variables interact with each other'. Generalizing or transferring models of bilingual education across different contexts is perilous, because this assumes that there is a magic formula for success.

(2) Readers can learn more about US bilingual education program models in the US: Sugarman, J. (2018) A matter of design: English learner program models in k-12 education. *Migration Policy Institute, Research Brief* Issue 2. See https://www.migratio npolicy.org/research/english-learner-program-models-k-12-education

(3) Coral Way K-8 Center, Miami, Florida is rated 'A' by the Florida Department of Education, based on student achievement data.

(4) The 1984 article is published with an accent mark in Richard's last name, as are some of his earlier writings. Later documents suggest that Richard did not want to use an accent mark on his surname (Smith, 2016).

References

Adams, D.W. (1995) *Education for Extinction: American Indians and the Boarding School Experience, 1875–1928*. Lawrence, KS: University Press of Kansas.

Baker, C. and Wright, W.E. (2017) *Foundations of Bilingual Education and Bilingualism* (6th edn). Bristol: Multilingual Matters.

Boyle, A., August, D., Tabaku, L., Cole, S. and Simpson-Baird, A. (2015) *Dual Language Education Programs: Current State Policies and Practices*. Office of English Language Acquisition. US Department of Education. December.

Coady, M. (2001) Policy and practice in bilingual education: Gaelscoileanna in the Republic of Ireland. Unpublished doctoral dissertation, University of Colorado, Boulder.

Coady, M. (2019) Florida's bilingual education. See www.bilingualeducationfl.org (accessed 1 June 2019).

Escamilla, K. (2018) Growing up with the Bilingual Education Act: One educator's journey. *Bilingual Research Journal* 41 (4), 369–387.

Feinberg, R.C. (2002) *Bilingual Education: A Reference Handbook*. Denver, CO: ABC-CLIO.

Florida Department of Education (2018) Data on English language learners and Florida's school districts. See http://www.fldoe.org/academics/eng-language-learners/ (accessed 1 June 2019).

Fránquiz, M., Escamilla, K. and Valdez, V. (2016) Introduction to special topics issue on Richard Ruiz. *Bilingual Research Journal* 39 (3-4), 167–172.

Gándara, P. (2015) Rethinking bilingual instruction. *Educational Leadership* 72 (6), 60–64.

García, O. (2009) *Bilingual Education in the 21st Century: A Global Perspective*. Malden, MA: John Wiley.

Granados, N. (2016) A letter to Richard Ruiz from a former student. *Bilingual Research Journal* 39 (3–4), 369.

Hornberger, N.H. (1991) Extending enrichment bilingual education: Revisiting typologies and redirecting policy. In O. García (ed.) *Bilingual Education: Focusschrift in Honor of Joshua A. Fishman on the Occasion of his 65th Birthday* (pp. 215–234). Philadelphia, PA: Benjamins.

Malpica, T. (2017) *Esa Mañana*. Miami, FL: Cuatro Gatos Press.

Mackey, W.F. and Beebe, V.N. (1977) *Bilingual Schools for a Bicultural Community: Miami's Adaptation to the Cuban Refugees*. Rowley, MA: Newbury House Publishers.

MacKinney, E. (2016) Language ideologies and bilingual realities: The case of Coral Way. In N. Hornberger (ed.) *Honoring Richard Ruiz and His Work on Language Planning and Bilingual Education* (pp. 301–315). Bristol: Multilingual Matters.

MacSwan, J., Thompson, M.S., Rolstad, K., McAlister, K. and Lobo, G. (2017) Three theories of the effects of language education programs: An empirical evaluation of bilingual and English-only policies. *Annual Review of Applied Linguistics* 37, 218–240. See https://doi.org/10.1017/S0267190517000137

McField, G.P. and McField, D.R. (2014) The consistent outcome of bilingual education programs: A meta-analysis of meta-analyses. In G.P. McField (ed.) *The Miseducation of English Learners* (pp. 267–298). Charlotte, NC: Information Age.

Otero, E. (2009) *El alfabeto cubano*. Autores Editores.

Ovando, C.J. (2003) Bilingual education in the United States: Historical development and current issues. *Bilingual Research Journal* 27 (1), 1–25.

Pellerano, C., Fradd, S.H. and Rovira, L. (1998) Coral Way Elementary School: A success story in bilingualism and biliteracy. *Discover, 3*. National Clearinghouse for Bilingual Education. Washington, DC.

Peterson, B. (2017) The struggle for bilingual education. In E. Barbian, G.C. Gonzales and P. Mejía (eds) *Rethinking Bilingual Education* (pp. 274–279). Milwaukee, WI: Rethinking Schools.

Richardson, M. (1964) An evaluation of certain aspects of the academic achievement of elementary pupils in a bilingual program. Unpublished dissertation proposal, University of Miami, Miami, FL.

Ruiz, R. (1984) Orientations in language planning. *NABE Journal* 8 (2), 15–34.

Ruiz, R. (1997) The empowerment of language-minority students. In A. Darder, R.D. Torres and H. Giroux (eds) *Latinos and Education: A Critical Reader* (pp. 319–328). New York: Routledge.

Smith, H. (2016) The orientations to language: The orientations to life. *Bilingual Research Journal* 39 (3–4), 365–366.

Stepick, A. and Stepick, C.D. (2009) Diverse contexts of reception and feelings of belonging. *Forum: Qualitative Social Research* 10 (3), Art 15. (np).

Sugarman, J. (2018) A matter of design: English learner program models in K-12 education. *Migration Policy Institute, Research Brief* Issue 2. Washington, DC. Retrieved from https://www.migrationpolicy.org/research/english-learner-program-models-k-1 2-education

Thomas, W.P. and Collier, V.P. (1997) *School Effectiveness for Language Minority Students*. Washington, DC: National Clearinghouse for English Language Acquisition.

University of Florida (2019) Coral Way. Digital Collections. Gainesville, FL. See http://ufdc.ufl.edu/coralway (accessed 1 July 2019).

Warhol, L. (2011) Native American language education as policy-in-practices: An interpretive policy analysis of the Native American Languages Act of 1990/1992.

International Journal of Bilingual Education and Bilingualism 14 (3), 279–299. doi: 10.1080/13670050.2010.486849

Wilson, D.M. (2011) Dual language programs on the rise: 'Enrichment' model puts content learning front and center for ELL students. *Harvard Education Letter* 27 (2). See http://hepg.org/hel-home/issues/27_2/helarticle/dual-language-programs-on-the-rise (accessed 1 July 2019).

Wright, W.E. (2019) *Foundations for Teaching English Language Learners: Research, Theory, Policy and Practice* (3rd edn). Philadelphia, PA: Caslon Publishing.

1 Origin of the Experiment

Cuban Exodus to the United States

Although Coral Way is a legacy in the field of bilingual education, known for its contribution to the use of two languages as mediums of instruction in school with students from different language backgrounds, the story of Coral Way begins as far back as January 1959, the month and year in which Fidel Castro descended from the mountainous countryside of Cuba and overthrew the Batista government. Little could anyone have known that a revolution on a small island country located 90 miles off the US coast that education in the United States would be fundamentally transformed for decades to come.

Early in 1959, the Castro regime, in power following then-President Batista's flee to Mexico, began implementing policies that ruptured the existing lifestyle of the majority of Cubans. Under the rule of the People's Socialist Party, Cubans on the island feared leftist, communist programs and policies being implemented. Many white-collar professionals on the island were sent to labor camps, despite their professional credentials. The Castro government wasted no time in closing down churches and banning clergy from practice. A staunchly Catholic country, many Cubans began to leave the island for fear of imprisonment and restrictions on their religious beliefs. Guerra (2012) reports that families who remained on the island also feared for the welfare and religious orientation of their children.

For many Cubans, Miami, Florida, was a logical destination during and after Castro's ascent to power. Increasing numbers of Cubans began to leave the island, many destined for Miami due to its proximity (less than 100 miles) and its social, economic and cultural connections to Cuba. Before Castro rose to power, Cubans frequently traveled to and maintained strong ties with the United States. Miami was considered the preferred vacation spot for the Cuban middle class and a place where affluent Cubans practiced their English and acquired business skills. Wealthy Cubans traveled to Miami for weekend shopping. Sandoval (1991: 6) notes that 'it was only natural [that] when the political oppression of Castro's regime set in, many chose Florida as the place to go' to wait out their imminent return to the island. However, the return to Cuba has not yet occurred.

Cubans seeking refuge in the United States received some financial backing and support from the US government. Guerra (2012) notes the financial influence that the US Central Intelligence Agency (CIA) provided to Cuban refugees in the early 1960s. She describes that between 1960 and 1965, the CIA distributed more than $50 million through their operating station located at the University of Miami. A report by Mitchell in 1966 indicated that the US government had been providing financial resettlement funding as early as 1961 under the Cuban Refugee Program (Mitchell, 1966), starting with about $1 million of presidential discretionary funding. Two of the nine major directives of the program included:

6. Furnish federal assistance for local public school operating costs related to the unforeseen impact of Cuban refugee children on local teaching facilities;
7. Initiate needed measures to augment training and educational opportunities for Cuban refugees, including physicians, teachers, and those with other professional backgrounds. (Mitchell, 1966: 3)

In 1961, the total amount of funding allocated to the Cuban Refugee Program was $4 million. While many Cubans sought ways to leave the island, the activities and economic aid of the US government played a role in supporting families' transition, including healthcare, professional retraining for employment, childcare, food distribution and housing. Guerra (2012) writes further that this amounted to a certain degree of enticement provided to Cubans to leave the island, with material supports put in place to ensure that Cubans would not have to struggle in ways that many other immigrant groups to the United States had previously.

Among the mass of people leaving Cuba were highly educated professionals, teachers and children. The education system in Cuba was acclaimed to be rigorous and of the highest standards, and scholars continue to note the benefits of the Cuban centralized education system (Carnoy et al., 2007).

One area where Cuban education excelled was in language teaching and learning. As early as the 1940s, the Cuban education system offered children and adults the opportunity to learn English as a foreign language. Rosa Guas Inclán, a professor at the University of Havana and a teacher at the American school, the Ruston Academy, founded the first Modern Foreign Language Association in Cuba. Inclán became a consultant to Florida's Dade County Public Schools (DCPS), preparing teachers to work with Spanish-speaking children. She ended up as a full-time administrator working for the school district and made significant contributions to recruiting and preparing Cuban teachers to work in DCPS. She was described by colleagues who worked with her as the ground force.

Another English language teacher who arrived in Miami after Castro came to power was Dr Josefina Sánchez Pando. Sánchez underscored the sentiment that emigrating Cubans were highly educated in the area of languages. She remarked that 'at the same time that in Miami nobody would be teaching Spanish, the Centro Especiales de Inglés, special English centers, existed in every other school in Havana in which English was taught to the population'.[1] Born in Cuba on 27 August 1927, Sánchez held a PhD in the field of education. Like other refugees who fled Cuba, Sánchez arrived in Miami in 1961 without papers or academic credentials, because the Cuban government would not allow documents to be taken out of the country. Sánchez described the high education standards that existed in Cuba in the mid-20th century, stating 'our standards of education were much higher than any other South or Central American country'.[2] She attributes the quality of education in Cuba to the influence of Europe, proudly reporting, 'we were a combination of... the best of Europe and the criollo... that had come out of the mixture and the acculturation of 200–300 years of excellent education in Cuba'.

Operation Pedro Pan

Adding to the increasing number of Cuban students in Dade schools was a clandestine operation that essentially smuggled children out of Cuba (Vidal de Haymes, 2004). Between 1960 and 1962, a largely unknown US-backed operation supported the emigration of Cuban children between the ages of 3 and 16 to the United States (Torres, 2003). The operation was called Peter Pan, or Operación Pedro Pan, titled subsequent to the arrival of a 15-year-old boy from Cuba named Pedro, who sought refuge and was provided assistance from the US-based Catholic Welfare Bureau.

Father Bryan Walsh, representing the Catholic Welfare Bureau, led the US-side of Operation Pedro Pan and his task was to ensure that Cuban children were housed and cared for on their arrival in the United States. Back in Havana, a British teacher at the Ruston Academy named Penny Powers, along with Polita Grau and her brother Ramon Grau organized visa paperwork and airline tickets for children to travel from Cuba to the United States. Their task included whiting out names and birth dates on existing visa waivers and reproducing the waivers for Cuban children to enter the United States legally (Bravo, 2010; Conde, 1999). They also produced passports for children to leave Cuba. Between 1961 and 1965, the group secured the exodus of more than 14,000 children and later obtained visas for the children's parents (Conde, 1999; Gonzalez-Pando, 2014). Polita and her brother were eventually tried for 'taking the youth out of Cuba' and for an alleged assassination attempt on Castro. They were each sentenced to 30 years in a Cuban prison of which Polita served 14 years (Gonzalez-Pando, 2014).

During Operation Pedro Pan, Cuban children up to 16 years old entered the United States alone and facing extremely unknown futures. Between 26 December 1960 and 23 October 1962, more than 14,000 parentless children were airlifted from Havana to Miami. Children arrived on flights twice daily: 3pm and 5pm. Those organizing the program both from Cuba and the United States and who were involved in Operation Pedro Pan strongly believed that the separation of parents and children was temporary and that the US government would soon overthrow the Castro regime (Torres, 2003; Vidal de Haymes, 2004). Vidal de Haymes described the harrowing experience of parents making the decision to separate from their children. Vidal de Haymes's brothers were sent to the United States first:

> The decision to send them ahead was made by my parents amid the rumors of a coming 'patria postetad,' a document that allegedly would order all children over the age of three into State care for the purposes of indoctrinating them with 'Castroism.' Fear of losing their children to the state made exiling their children an attractive option for many Cuban parents, including mine who sent my brothers to the U.S. through the Pedro Pan (Peter Pan) program. (Vidal de Haymes, 2004: 120)

The experiences of the Pedro Pan children who arrived in the United States without their families was socially and emotionally devastating. The children missed their parents, families, support network, culture and language. Some children spent significant time in orphanages in South Florida; others were temporarily adopted by host families and relocated around the United States. Some of the stories of the Pedro Pan children have found their way into popular literature. Carlos Eire (2004), for instance, described his experiences leaving his parents in Havana and landing in Miami, only to be ushered to a Catholic camp run by nuns in Homestead, Florida. Separated from his older brother, Tony, at Miami airport, Eire (2004: 343) writes, 'we were loaded into different vans and taken to different camps.

Tony went to a camp for teens in Kendall, and I went to a camp for pre-teens in Homestead'. Eventually, Carlos and Tony were 'adopted' by different families living in close proximity to one another in Miami. What ensues in Eire's book are his childhood experiences, how he makes sense of what happened, where he came from and who he subsequently became.

Sánchez recalls children arriving in Miami, being 'adopted' by local families, and her attempt to help them in the lonely transition. She took it as her personal mission to help children who had arrived alone in a foreign country without family or personal belongings:

> I would go to [house] and [house] and pick up the kids and I would take them to catechism, to church. We would go to Key Biscayne, which was under development at that time, with some bait and some thread, and we would fish, right there. I could take them out at night, and we would all bring a big, big towel, sit on the sand, and look up at the stars and study the constellations, and think of the differences of movement in the stars.[3]

Sánchez recalls telling the children, 'Now, if you write Mommy in your next letter, that three weeks from today we're going to be here, lying on the sand, looking at the constellations. If they do the same thing over there, we could talk. We could look at the stars, and you could tell your Mommy and your Daddy how you miss them'.

Early Bilingual Educators of the Coral Way Bilingual Program

In 1961, Josefina Sánchez Pando arrived in Miami from Havana. Aiming to register her daughter for elementary school, she crossed the main entrance of Coral Way Elementary School and entered the front door. Having been an English teacher in Cuba, Sánchez's English was impeccable. She immediately saw the need to assist the office staff in registering the line of Spanish-speaking children, and Sánchez began to interpret for school staff on the spot. Within two weeks of entering the school, Sánchez was hired by the principal and began working at Coral Way as one of the first Cuban aides.

Her recollection of the two years before Coral Way was identified as the site for the experimental bilingual program, was one of welcoming, caring and nurturing:

> [t]he support was magnificent. I have never in my life seen a PTA as those first PTAs. The things they gave the children, the parties they gave them, the lot of love they gave them. We went to everything that existed here. The field trips they paid for. They took those children around.[4]

Sánchez recalls the empathy that developed in the local community, the desperation of the children who missed their families and the 'love' she describes that the people gave to the children. She recalls that

> most everybody that was here at the time had had some big catastrophe happen in their own family, and the empathy was enormous, because I could feel how Esperanza was desperate to see her mother—because I didn't have my mother either here…. I taught them how to look at the grass, and the beauty of the flowers that hide under the grass. Because we had nothing.[5]

A second teacher, María 'Tita' Piñeiro, also arrived in Miami following the Cuban revolution and was among the first Cuban aides to work in schools in Miami in 1961 along with Sánchez. Her work was to assist the English-speaking staff and teachers with the influx of Cuban children arriving daily. She worked in the orientation classes, which aimed to transition children into local schools. She recalls that the classes were overwhelmed, 'because every day two flights from Havana were arriving'.[6]

A third important educator from Cuba was Rosa Guas Inclán. Inclán was born in Cuba and was sister of Rafael Guas Inclán, former vice president of Cuba (1954–1958). Inclán was remembered as the leader on the ground in Dade County schools who began to identify Cuban teachers from Miami as possible Cuban aides. She was the force behind mobilizing the Cuban aides to obtain teacher credentials in Florida through the University of Miami Cuban Teacher Retraining Project (Feinberg, 1999). In her work describing the Coral Way bilingual program, Inclán (1979: 16) recounted the need in Miami in 1960–1962 to identify 'Cuban educators who had extensive experience in Cuba training ESL teachers teaching in bilingual school settings and adapting or developing appropriate instructional materials in ESL for diverse levels and diverse student needs'. Those were the foundational skills sought out by Inclán and Dade County schools for teachers who could work in the Coral Way bilingual program.

The number of Cuban refugee students entering DCPS between 1959 and 1962 escalated. Mackey and Beebe note that in 1960, about 5000 students with a Cuban background participated in education in DCPS, primarily located in the city boundaries of Miami. According to García and Otheguy (1985), some of the early new arrivals to Miami were the children of wealthy Cubans, who attended local private schools. With the continuous flow of Cuban children leaving the island, including under Operation Pedro Pan, the number of Spanish-speaking children in Dade

County schools increased from approximately 8,700 in September 1961 to 18,260 in September 1962, an increase of approximately 110% in one year (Mackey & Beebe, 1977).

The Emergence of a Visionary

The large number of Cuban children was not without local consequences and social and political tensions, and the Dade County school district had the difficult task of providing education to these students. As noted in the Prologue of this book, language ideologies – that is, beliefs about language and language use – are inextricably intertwined with national and individual identity and the process of education. Dade County schools were subject to these ideologies. As Dade County began to address the need for first language instruction for Cuban refugee children, pressure mounted. Dr Pauline Martz Rojas, a formidable educator with a national reputation as a highly skilled linguist (Mackey & Beebe, 1977), was hired by Dade County school district to address the language and educational pressures.

The district's two primary and immediate educational concerns were the need for appropriate teaching materials to teach Spanish-speaking children in all-English classrooms, and to prepare English-speaking teachers to teach Spanish-speaking Cuban children.[7] The district also understood the social effects of the Cuban political situation and its implications for American families and children. Their concerns about the social effects were conveyed to the Ford Foundation. In their internal memorandums in 1961, the Ford Foundation noted the acuity of the DCPS situation:

10,000 Cuban children in the Dade county schools and the number is increasing weekly. The school system is not able to handle in any satisfactory way the most fundamental problems posed by this large scale immigration, namely the language problem… the ratio of students to teachers is rapidly getting out of hand. An equally serious problem concerns the American children in the school system. Many classes are far behind in their school work as a result of the influx of Cuban children who know no English but who are placed in the same classes. Parents of these American children have begun to put pressure on the school boards to segregate the pupils in different schools.[8]

Pauline Rojas conveyed this information to the Ford Foundation. Rojas was hired as a consultant by DCPS Superintendent Joe Hall in September 1961 to identify a solution to the Cuban refugee situation. Rojas was a former bilingual English as a second language (ESL) teacher and earned her degree from the University of Puerto Rico, where she married Puerto Rican, Antonio Rojas (Mackey & Beebe, 1977). She was a consultant with the Center for Applied Linguistics (CAL) in Washington, DC, and traveled extensively, learning about bilingual education programs around the world. At the time of the Cuban exodus in 1960, Rojas was working at the Office of Education in Miami, setting up an institute to teach English to Cuban refugees who had enlisted in the US Armed Forces.[9] With a reputation as a knowledgeable and 'outstanding' linguist,[10] Rojas resigned her position with the US Armed Forces because the program numbers were diminishing, and joined DCPS.

Rojas spent the first six weeks in her new position studying the educational situation. She noted that approximately 250–300 new students arrived in Dade schools each week. Before the end of her first month with DCPS, Rojas traveled to Washington, DC, to meet with education officials at the US Office of Health, Education and Welfare. Her goal was to make known the large-scale problem that Dade County was facing and to identify funding for the district.[11] Rojas left Washington in late 1961 without any financial commitment or additional federal funding. However, her networking did build professional connections. Ken Mildenberger, who headed the Language Development Program at the US Office of Education at the time,[12] suggested to Rojas that she contact the Ford Foundation as a possible solution for Dade County's educational needs. Mildenberger recommended that Rojas contact James Tierney who worked at the Ford Foundation offices in New York. Before leaving the northeast on that fateful trip, Rojas walked into the foundation offices and secured a meeting with Tierney on 29 September 1961.[13]

The Orientation Program: Foreground to the Bilingual Program

While Rojas was networking for national support for the DCPS crisis, the situation in Dade schools continued to deteriorate. By November 1961, DCPS stated that it was 'at the crossroads' and needed to develop a plan to address the educational needs of Cuban student refugees.[14] Under Rojas's guidance, the district designed and released a plan, 'Basic Program for Cuban Pupils', to schools in the district. The program consisted of a set of guidelines – including a sizeable list of do's and don'ts – for teachers working with Spanish-speaking Cuban students. Under Rojas's leadership, the district's short-term solution to the problem was to establish an 'orientation teacher' at each school with a large number of Cuban students and to provide those teachers with professional development.

In the plan, an orientation teacher was defined as 'any teacher who has a Cuban aide under his/her supervision or who teaches English as a second language'.[15] The orientation teachers had four main tasks:

(1) To help Spanish-speaking children to adjust to school life in Miami.
(2) To teach them English.
(3) To help other teachers understand the problems of the Spanish-speaking children.
(4) To advise administrators on the daily programs, textbooks, adjustment problems, etc., of these children.[16]

Cuban aides were educated bilinguals who were hired by DCPS to assist orientation teachers. Many of the aides were qualified teachers in Cuba, noted earlier by Inclán, but the state of Florida did not recognize their credentials. Under the Basic Program for Cuban Pupils, Cuban aides were prohibited from working with Cuban students who had higher language proficiency levels in English. Their role was primarily to support 'non-independent' students who had little or no knowledge of English in regular classrooms. In an article describing the relationship between the early Dade County orientation program from 1960 to 1962 and the establishment of the bilingual program, Inclán (1980: 6) noted, '[t]he orientation classes were really the beginning of bilingual education, for the American teachers would provide language arts (English as a second language), math, art, music and physical education in English, while the Cuban aides would provide language arts and other subjects in Spanish'.

The Plan for the Bilingual Program

As the orientation program grew with the increasing numbers of Cuban refugee children, Rojas continued to communicate with the Ford Foundation and with Dr Edward J. Meade in particular. DCPS was encouraged to submit a proposal to Ford. While the orientation teacher program was being rolled out across the district, Dade County Superintendent Joseph Hall worked with Rojas to submit a three- to five-year proposal to the Ford Foundation that would provide a more comprehensive approach and medium-term solutions to support the Cuban students and American teachers. Rojas returned to the Ford Foundation in New York in November 1961, following the superintendent's endorsement of a plan to (a) develop teaching materials for Cuban students learning ESL and (b) prepare teachers to teach ESL to those students.

The initial comprehensive project proposed by Hall had two main subprojects. The first subproject was to provide instructional materials to teachers such as pre-primers, charts and visual aids for Spanish-speaking students in DCPS. The second subproject was to adapt what was then one of the few, if any, ESL reading materials, the *Fries American English Series*.[17] A memo from Hall on 28 November 1961 appealed to Ford for $98,500 (the equivalent of $815,000 in 2018 dollars) to initiate the two objectives. In his letter, Hall wrote, 'since we are faced daily with making decisions regarding the operation of an educational program for these growing numbers of Cuban refugee pupils, we are in urgent need of your help at the earliest possible moment'.[18]

Meade summarized Hall's request and his ongoing communications with Rojas in a memo to Dr Alvin Eurich. Eurich was the executive director of Ford Foundation's Educational Division and oversaw proposals for funding. In his memo, Meade noted the seriousness of the situation and the capability of Dade County to adequately use the funding under the leadership of Dr Pauline Rojas who was considered a 'pro' in the field of linguistics. Meade summarized the Dade County request into four objectives:

1. a two-way public relations program to help the English-speaking and Spanish-speaking members of the community to learn to understand and appreciate each other;
2. conversion of a certain number of elementary and junior high schools into truly bilingual schools in which all pupils would study in the two languages;
3. organization of a production staff of language specialists who would prepare and program materials for English teaching and Spanish teaching. [sic] and
4. organization of a supervisory staff who would visit school personnel to give demonstration classes, and try out materials.

As Ford Foundation executives studied the issue, they decided that requests (1) and (2) were 'a lesser priority' for funding and that requests (3) and (4) should be the basis for Ford Foundation support to DCPS. The initial plan to create multiple bilingual education programs where students would be educated through the medium of two languages was rejected by Ford Foundation executives.

Funding for the Bilingual Program

Rojas and Hall's perseverance started to pay off. Ford Foundation executive Meade and Rojas continued to discuss the foundation's support for Dade County schools. Rojas traveled to New York on at least two occasions where she met with Meade, and Meade was invited to Miami to visit schools in January 1962. Finally, Meade received an updated proposal from Dade Superintendent Joe Hall that same month, and he seemed to understand the urgency in Dade County. In an internal Ford Foundation memo, Meade persuaded Eurich:

Forget for the moment that we are dealing with a problem of immediate concern. Dade County is not seeking support to bail them out. We are not being asked to provide support to help solve a local problem. What we are being asked to consider is the possibility of helping to support the development of a long-range solution which would have educational significance nationally. At the present time, there is an ever-growing practice of teaching foreign languages along the lines of the aural-oral approach. At the same time, there is no organized program fully committed to teach English in a similar fashion, yet in many schools throughout the land there are numbers of youngsters who come to school without any facility in the English language.[19] (emphasis retained)

The timing of the request was essential, because the goals aligned with the Ford Foundation's objectives of advancing foreign area studies and foreign language programs, particularly through its International Training and Research Program (Beckmann, 1964). In the prior decade, Ford had spent more than $138 million (in 1960s dollars) to 'improve American competence to deal with international problems' (Beckmann, 1964: 15).

Meade summarized the forthcoming Dade County proposal to the Ford Foundation in four areas: the development of materials to teach English as a language to primary-grade students; the concurrent development of methods to use those materials in schools; the concurrent revision of the *Fries American English Series* for intermediate- and secondary-level students; and 'the start of a bilingual education program for the elementary school'.[20] To the last point on bilingual education, Meade ended the memo with 'I don't anticipate the expectancy for outside funds to help support this part of the program at this time'. In other words, Ford was not expected to support the development of a bilingual education program.

On 26 January 1962, Dade County revised and resubmitted its proposal to the Ford Foundation, requesting $278,000 from Ford and committing $153,600 from Dade County funds to engage in the four areas. The final proposal had 13 stated objectives but they focused their proposal on the development and adaptation of ESL materials, and teacher education for ESL students. Although none of the proposed funded objectives related to the establishment of a bilingual education program, Dade County noted that one implication of the materials and teacher development *could* be the establishment of such a school for 'future development'.[21] Ford agreed to the proposal based on the two focus areas.

Communication between Ford and Dade County continued from February through June 1962 as Dade County waited for feedback from Ford on their proposal. At the same time, some early funding from the US government on the Cuban crises, through the Cuban Refugee Program (Mitchell, 1962), began to make its way into Dade County schools. Yet, the urgency of the situation in Dade County continued to increase, and Meade aimed to keep the proposal alive. Early that summer, however, the Ford Foundation decided to defer its decision from June 1962 until the fall. Meade communicated with Hall and described the delay as due to internal Ford Foundation affairs. To assuage Hall's concerns, Meade commented that other proposals for Ford Foundation consideration were similarly tabled to a later date. Following the deferral, Meade traveled to Miami in September 1962 and spent two days at the district offices reviewing the district's proposal on-site. The meeting must have impressed Meade, because subsequent to his return to New York, Dade County submitted a revised proposal to Ford, now the third version, on 24 September 1962. Finally, the much awaited, discussed and negotiated project for $278,000 was approved, and the two main objectives were set: to create materials for teaching English using the Fries series as a foundation for ESL students, and to prepare teachers for English-learning students. There was no commitment to bilingual education.

The Coral Way Bilingual Program

Pauline Rojas was the visionary who led the charge for Dade County schools and for Spanish-speaking Cuban students. She not only had experience working in ESL contexts, but she also knew reading methods and understood the role of literacy development in second language learning. Rojas also had a vision for bilingual education programs in Dade County schools. The initial proposal to Ford included a vision for multiple bilingual programs throughout schools in Dade County, but that was essentially rejected by Ford. The final funded proposal to Ford was crafted by Rojas and her colleague Paul Bell. Bell was a former ESL teacher in Guatemala with experience in curriculum development. Their proposal was titled 'Project in the Bilingual Education of Cuban Refugee Pupils'.

Mackey and Beebe (1977) state that there was some evidence to suggest that Rojas's inspiration for the bilingual education program derived from a Spanish–English bilingual school that she observed in Guayaquil, Ecuador.[22]

Although the establishment of a bilingual education program at the elementary level was not at the forefront of the proposal and funding from the Ford Foundation, it was very much so for Rojas. Internal archives from DCPS indicate that the four main tasks to be accomplished with funding from the Ford Foundation included:

(1) the preparation of reading materials for non-English-speaking bilingual pupils entering first grade;
(2) the revision or adaptation of the books of the *Fries American English Series* for non-English-speaking bilingual pupils who can read and write their vernacular;
(3) the preparation of guides and audiovisual materials for teachers of bilingual pupils;
(4) the establishment of a bilingual school.

However, internal memoranda between Ford Foundation executives Meade and Eurich stressed that Ford funding might 'pave the way'[23] for a future bilingual school, but it was not something that Ford funds would support directly. Thus, Ford funding was not to be used for establishing the bilingual program, but the ESL materials and teacher education may eventually contribute to the program.

To begin the program, Rojas assembled a strong team of educators with a plan to carry out the work. Rojas, whose title changed to director of the Ford-funded program, hired Bell to provide on-the-ground support for the program. The second order of business was to determine which school site, students and teachers would participate in the bilingual school experiment. Rojas wanted the number of Spanish and English speakers to be about 50%, and she also needed Spanish bilingual teachers and English-speaking teachers to share the same 50:50 ratio. Her plan was for academic instruction to be 50% in each language for both groups of students. These are two cornerstones of a '50:50' model of a 'two-way immersion' (TWI) bilingual education program (García, 2009).

García (2009: 130) notes that TWI bilingual programs are also referred to as 'dual-language' programs, which, she states, avoids the 'politics surrounding the ideologically loaded "bilingual"' term. The goal of bilingual education programs from a language perspective is to develop high degrees of bilingualism and biliteracy for all participating students. From a cultural perspective, the programs aim for bicultural-ism, a somewhat amorphous term that captures the complex ability of students to understand and navigate within and across different cultural groups. Bilingual-bicultural students are sometimes considered adept cultural brokers (Dorner *et al.*, 2007).

Funding from the Ford Foundation began to flow into Dade County schools in early January 1963. Rojas identified Mr Ralph Robinett who had experience as a teacher in Puerto Rico and as an ESL specialist with the Puerto Rican Department of Education, and agreed to manage the Ford project only with the support of Robinett, whom she trusted and with whom she had worked producing the *Fries American English Series*, which was used as an ESL reading curriculum in Puerto Rico.[24] Rojas oversaw the big picture of the Ford project and set the course for the work, and Robinett, along with Bell, worked 'on the ground' with school administrators and teachers.

The final committed Ford Foundation funding was $278,000 distrib-uted over a three-year period. It provided financial support with four specific, action-oriented goals: the preparation of reading materials for non-English-speaking students entering first grade; the adaptation of the *Fries American English Series* books for non-English-speaking students; the preparation of guides and audiovisual materials for teachers of bilin-gual students; and the establishment of a bilingual school.[25] In current dollars, the Ford Foundation grant equated to more than $2.1 million, a sizeable three-year investment in education in south Florida and in Dade County schools in particular.

Perhaps it was the constellation of the abrupt political change, a highly educated Cuban populace and the deep empathy for the thousands of Cuban children who landed in Miami that contributed to a positive 'context of reception' for Cubans. Stepick and Stepick (2009) describe the context of reception as

> how the established residents of the host society perceive and categorize newcomers affects migrants' sense of belonging. This is not only a one way street. The presence of migrants as neighbors, workers and school-mates in communities often elicits reflections on established residents' own sense of belonging and rights of belonging. (Stepick & Stepick, 2009: 1)

The positive context of reception experienced by Cubans, particularly parentless children, undoubtedly contributed to an atmosphere of oppor-tunity and, in the case of Coral Way, experimentation. Adding to this sentiment, Ovando (2003) notes that Cubans generally experienced low levels of racism due to having primarily light skin.

In response to the urgent need for educational solutions, some additional factors converged between 1961 and 1962 that contributed to the solutions devised by Rojas to support Dade County schools and the Cuban refugee children. Those factors included a highly prepared Spanish–English bilingual teaching force; a positive context of reception and sense of altruism for Cuban refugee children separated from their parents under Operation Pedro Pan; an active, persistent bilingual leader with expertise in language and education and a vision for a solution; and external funding to support the development and implementation of an educational innovation. The combination of events – the history of Cubans in the area, the reception of Cuban children following their ordeal leaving Cuba, federal financial assistance, racial similarities to white English speakers and the temporary condition of sojourners in Miami led to an opportunistic moment. In this broad social and political context, both English and Spanish could be considered resources for learning. How much learning, however, was yet to be examined.

The Coral Way Community

While Rojas was working on a plan to provide support to Dade County for the Cuban students, the neighborhood surrounding Coral Way was experiencing an increase in the number of Spanish-speaking children. A traditional English-speaking neighborhood with a school of about 750 students, the number of Spanish speakers began to rise steadily through 1961 and 1962 (Mackey & Beebe, 1977). Sánchez recalls that the children who arrived had very few material items, with some arriving in Miami without adequate clothing for the winter. Piñeiro, like other teachers, echoed the welcoming sentiment and positive reception from members of the Coral Way community. 'The secretary [of Coral Way] was a volunteer at the Baptist church around the corner. When children needed shoes', she recalled, 'Principal Logan would announce it on the loud speaker in the morning. "Okay, we need more shoes" or "we need more of this"'.[26] The community became active.

The neighborhood's Jewish community played an important role both in terms of the reception of students from Cuba and in the development of bilingualism. The neighborhood surrounding the Coral Way school was strongly Jewish, and students who attended Coral Way attended Beth David synagogue two afternoons each week and learned Hebrew. Piñeiro described that 'the Jewish community was the number one accepting us, because the families knew what they went through... we were like a big family'.[27]

In addition to working at the school as a Cuban aide, Sánchez taught Spanish at night during 1961 and 1962 to English-speaking adults, many of whom spoke Yiddish in the home and learned Hebrew at the synagogue. The neighborhood surrounding the school was ethnically diverse and seemed receptive to multilingual language use. Some of the Jewish families temporarily adopted incoming children and families in their homes. But Sánchez describes that there were economic reasons, 'they were merchants... They knew that the United States had to look to South America and Central America for markets. They knew that money would be coming up and down, and going up and down South America and Central America. And they also knew that if they could speak the language, they could sell... their products'.[28] The solidly middle-class neighborhood with welcoming multilingual families seemed ripe for the bilingual experiment.

The relationship between the Jewish community and the Cubans seemed mainly symbiotic. Sánchez described the Jewish community as 'our backbones, because they knew of the importance of more than one language, because they taught their children Yiddish and they went to Hebrew school, and they knew more than one language, English plus "A", "B", or "C"'. She attributes the growth of the bilingual program as much to the Jewish community as to the Cuban immigrants who began to build businesses and social organizations, '[a]nd it started. The spark came out from the school and the children into the community'.[29]

The community began to experience financial expansion and economic benefits from the number of incoming Cubans and their determination to build new lives, even if temporary. They opened drugstores and hospitals, and some highly educated Cubans, who were initially unable to obtain employment in higher-paying jobs, found new opportunities in the area. Sánchez felt that among the existing community, particularly the Jewish families and merchants, learning languages meant that the two groups could 'be equals'.[30]

Cuban Aides

Cuban-trained teachers and professionals played a crucial role in Dade County schools between 1960 and 1962. The aides were already trained bilingual teachers, but as they lacked a Florida teaching credential, Dade County would not hire them directly as teachers. Under the 1961 plan designed by Rojas for orientation teachers, Cuban aides were responsible for Spanish-speaking students who performed at the 'non-independent' English language ability level in regular classroom settings. Non-independent pupils, according to DCPS guidelines, were those students not born in the United States who were beginning-level English learners and whose proficiency in English 'impeded the progress of the class'.[31] The district experienced increasing tension in regular classrooms that had a large number of non-English-speaking Cuban refugee students. American teachers were overwhelmed and parents began to complain.

Under the orientation program, Dade County recognized two levels of English language ability in addition to 'non-independent': independent students and intermediate students. Independent students were described as having enough English language ability to participate in – or at least not interfere with – regular classroom instruction. Intermediate-level students fell somewhere in between non-independent- and independent-level students. In the program, Cuban aides were strictly prohibited from working with Cuban students who performed at the independent level, because they were sorely needed to work with students at lower English language ability levels. In addition to rolling out the first Dade County plan to address Cuban student refugees, in November 1961, Rojas headed up an in-service education professional development program for teachers who were working with Cuban students.

Coral Way Elementary as the Bilingual Program Site

Coral Way Elementary had not yet been named as 'the' experimental bilingual school in January 1963, when the Ford Foundation grant officially began. Robinett was instructed to spend time familiarizing himself with Dade County schools in general and with 'Cuban refugee' students in particular. It wasn't until late spring of 1963 that Coral Way Elementary was selected as the site of the bilingual program. Three reasons prompted the selection of Coral Way. First, Cuban immigrant children continued to arrive in the neighborhood, which was beginning to approximate 50% Spanish speaking and 50% English speaking. In addition, there was a sense of economic stability, as noted earlier, with established families and a business-minded Jewish community. Mackey and Beebe (1977) describe the site's selection as based on the linguistic and economic characteristics of the neighborhood. They note that many of the area's Spanish-speaking residents 'had been successful businessmen and professionals in Cuba. Most had already achieved middle-income status in the United States and spoke some English... [and the] English-speaking citizens' socio-economic status ranged from the lower to the upper strata' (Mackey & Beebe, 1977: 63).

Second, the neighborhood was considered stable, with no low-income areas *per se*. Families in the community were considered middle class and settled rather than transient, hosting children arriving from Cuba daily in their homes. In short, families in the Coral Way neighborhood could afford to house additional children. Sánchez quipped that Coral Way was chosen because the families' houses were 'big enough to add another bed, to have another child'.

Third, the school community, parents, school administration and staff were enthusiastic about providing bilingual education for local children. J. Lee Logan, the principal of Coral Way Elementary, who began in that role in 1960, led local school efforts. He is frequently referred to as a champion of the program, enthusiastic and committed. Enthusiasm for the program needed to equate with strong and active school leadership, which were characteristics that Logan appeared to possess.

Will it Work? An Experimental Design

The Coral Way experiment was designed as an innovative educational program. In order to determine the effectiveness of the program on students' learning in English and in Spanish, a quasi-experimental design was proposed[32] and organized. Unlike true experimental designs in the social sciences, where participants are randomly assigned to a treatment, such as participating in a special instructional program, a quasi-experimental design does not randomly assign students. Instead, it matches the participants' background characteristics such as gender, race, ethnicity and socioeconomic status with a group of participants with similar characteristics who do not participate in the program (Cohen *et al.*, 2011). The background matching allows for analyses to be conducted that demonstrate the effects of the program on the participants. In the case of Coral Way, the comparisons across different groups of students would be made on their academic achievement using standardized tests.

To ensure that the bilingual education program was adequately designed and implemented following quasi-experimental design procedures, some notable scholars and consultants were named in the early report to the Ford Foundation, including Dr Charles Ferguson, the director of CAL in Washington, DC; Dr Theodore Clymer, president of the International Reading Association; Dr C.C. Fries, a retired English linguist from the University of Michigan, who wrote the original Fries series; and Dr Ross Macdonald, an English linguist working on machine translation in Washington, DC. Rojas knew several of the consultants personally and quickly garnered support for the experiment to take place. The Dade County school board considered the experiment during its meeting on 6 March 1963. The funding from the Ford Foundation, which had been informally approached by Dr Rojas and formally applied for by Dr Hall, the Dade superintendent, was already flowing into the district. In addition, the proposal to Ford had already determined early goals (development of materials, adaptation and use of the Fries series and establishment of a bilingual school). Hence, it seems that the Dade County school board's actions and approval of the program were just a formality. The following extended excerpt of the minutes from 6 March 1963 is noteworthy:

29,157: Authorize Experiment with Bilingual School During 1963–64 School Year

A memorandum was received from Mr. Robert B. Turner, Jr., Assistant Superintendent for General Education, and Miss Betty Gilkey, Director of Elementary Education, stating that the enrollment of large numbers of Spanish-speaking pupils in many elementary schools affords an opportunity which could be mutually beneficial to both the Spanish-speaking child and the English-speaking child.

They therefore recommend that an experiment with a bilingual school be initiated during the school year 1963–64. This experimental program to be operated in conjunction with the project to develop instructional materials for Cuban Refugees. The purpose would be to assist English-speaking pupils to speak, read, and write in both languages, and to assist Spanish-speaking pupils maintain literacy in Spanish as well as to learn English... ultimately it would be expected that about half of the instruction would be given in English and half in Spanish.

If this experimental program is approved, it will then be necessary to form a committee of teachers and supervisors of bilingual education to organize materials to be used by the teacher and pupils in this program.

Upon recommendation of the Superintendent, Mr. Robert B. Turner, Jr., and Miss Betty Gilkey, Mr. Gordon moved, seconded by Mr. Braddock and unanimously carried that an experiment with a bilingual school as outlined above, be initiated during the school year 1963–1964.[33]

The Dade County school board approved the Coral Way experiment on 6 March 1963. In no way was the experiment the result of a threat to public education in Dade County, due to Cuban children's parents' preference for private schools. Readers should also take note of the 'seconded' action by school board member, Mr Braddock, and the unanimous passing of the proposal.

Like other educational programs, this program was not without controversy later on, but the initial reception for the program seemed positive.[34] It wasn't until five weeks later, after the school board approval, that Principal Logan addressed the English-speaking parents of first- and second-grade students in a letter dated 14 April 1963. Logan described the opportunity that could be 'mutually beneficial' to both Spanish- and English-speaking students. He cautiously approached the gradual increase in language of instruction, describing how students would 'progress as rapidly as they are able to work comfortably'. Parents were given a set date to meet at the school lunchroom (Wednesday 24 April 1963) and a week from the date of the letter to indicate their interest in the 'unusual opportunity' for their child.[35]

The outcomes expected from the experiment focused on the students who participated in bilingual instruction following the proposed 50:50 model and a group of matched students who did not. The Coral Way experiment was not limited to student learning outcomes alone. Rather, Rojas and the Ford-funded group aimed to understand the intercultural communication skills of students, their social integration and their contributions to society. This seems contradictory to the temporary nature of the original Cuban immigrants' intentions of returning to Cuba. However, as Conde (1999) notes, the more time passed, the less likely it appeared that Cubans in the United States would return to their homeland.

Seven goals of the bilingual program

Once Coral Way was named the school site, the goals of the program were detailed. Rojas and her team believed that graduates of the program would benefit from enhanced job opportunities (see [6] in the following list), signaling that the financial benefits were very much on the minds of the experiment's designers. In order to evaluate the effectiveness of the program, the following seven metrics were established:

1. The participating pupil will have achieved as much in the way of skills, abilities, and understandings as he would have had he attended a monolingual school.
2. He will be approximately as proficient in his second language (within his educational level) as he is in his first language. If he is a skilled reader in his first language, he will be a skilled reader in

his second language. If he has mastered the fundamental processes and concepts in arithmetic in one language, he will handle them equally in the second language. If he can express himself clearly and adequately in his first language, he will be able to do likewise in the other language. If he understands and uses concepts in science and social studies, he will handle these concepts equally in both languages.

3. He will be able to operate in either culture easily and comfortably.
4. He will have acquired consciously or unconsciously an understanding of the symbolic nature of language and as a result will be able to achieve greater objectivity in his thinking processes.
5. In general terms, he will be more acceptive of strange people and cultures and will thus increase the range of his job opportunities.
6. He will have skills, abilities and understandings that will greatly extend his vocational potential and thus increase his usefulness to himself and the world in which he lives.
7. He will broaden his understanding of people and the world and be able to live a richer, fuller and more satisfying personal life.[36]

The ultimate four goals of cross-cultural communication – intercultural relationships, economic benefits, personal satisfaction and social contributions – were long-term, qualitative measures that could not be determined during the early years of the experiment and were outside of the quasi-experimental design, at least in the short and medium term. However, importantly, based on the objectives of the Coral Way experiment, five of the seven early goals did not rely on student achievement data to determine the effectiveness of the program. Instead, the outcomes and goals of the experiment were significantly more far-reaching.

Most of the benchmarks for success of the program were qualitative and would be difficult to ascertain, for instance, in today's educational environment of academic standards and standardized testing. Rojas and the Dade County school staff nevertheless emphasized the cross-cultural competence of the students, the intercultural relationships that the program hoped to develop, a sense of job or economic advancement for students who participated and, ultimately, students' larger contribution to society. Despite these emphases and goals in the original proposal to the Ford Foundation, there seemed to be no strategy to actually measure student satisfaction in the short term, nor to follow students longitudinally over a long period of time to determine if they had, indeed, attained satisfying lives.

Quantitative measures

Only two out of seven of the early objectives involved measurements of the students' language and literacy proficiency in English and Spanish. The first measure (see [1] in metrics list) aligned the Spanish- and English-speaking students who participated in Coral Way with Spanish- and English-speaking students who did not participate in Coral Way. For this measure, data on student learning needed to be collected from the students both in the bilingual program and from students with similar demographic backgrounds.

Although student achievement data from the experiment do not name the match sample site of students, Sánchez recalled that Auburndale Elementary was chosen as the comparison or 'parent school' in the quasi-experimental design. Located three miles from Coral Way, students at Auburndale Elementary had similar demographic characteristics in terms of parental income and it was a neighborhood school too. Sánchez describes the design of the experiment:

> Auburndale Elementary would do the same thing to the children that were there, [but] in English, English, English, English, English, English. Dump 'em into English... sink or swim. Let's see, in three years, what has come out of those children, how much English have they learned, and how much subject matter? Do they know social studies? Do they know science? Do they know the curriculum of the fifth-grade science? Was the language barrier strong enough to prevent those children from learning?[37]

The intent was to follow the first class of students in the program for three full years, from 1963 through 1966, and to assess their knowledge of social studies, science and mathematics. For Auburndale Elementary students, the assessments included academic content knowledge for Spanish-speaking students only.[38] The 'additional benefits' that the team intended to measure in achievement measure (1) were ambiguous, but the daily newspaper, *The Miami Herald*, portrayed the Coral Way program as innovative and 'bucking the one-language tradition'.[39] There was no intention to compare the performance of English-speaking students from Coral Way with English speakers from another school such as Auburndale.

Pragmatically, two measures of comparison needed to be conducted. First was the English-speaking students' academic progress measured by the widely used Achievement Test (SAT) in reading and mathematics, with students from Coral Way and students from Auburndale. Second was the Spanish-speaking students' academic progress measured using the SAT in reading and mathematics from students attending Coral Way and Auburndale, the match sample group.

The second measure (see [2] in metrics list) aimed to examine only students who participated in the Coral Way experiment but not compared with students enrolled in any other school. The second measure sought to determine 'if and at what point' students in the experiment would become bilingual (Table 1.1). This assessment measure referred to the concept of 'balanced bilingualism' in which an individual's language ability level in two languages is similar or 'balanced'. Balanced bilingualism refers to the development of bilingual competence in speaking, thinking, reading and writing to a degree of 'equivalent fluency' in both languages (Reyes *et al.*, 2012: 308), with some importance placed on literacy – reading and writing – development across both languages. Scholars of bilingualism (Gaardner, 1965; Grosjean, 1989; Schiffman, 1987) have long noted that balanced bilingualism is a concept that is pragmatically difficult to achieve.

Thus, the leaders of the Coral Way experiment, including Rojas, Robinett, Bell and the district office wanted to know if students' language abilities in English and Spanish were relatively equivalent after participating in the program for three years. In other words, would two languages used for academic instruction following a 50:50 model produce bilinguals who were more proficient in one language than another, or would participating students become more 'balanced' across the two languages over that period of time? With the unanimous Dade County school board vote came the promise of a new, exciting and untested chapter of education in the United States.

Table 1.1 Achievement measures of the Coral experiment

Goal	Purpose	Achievement measures
(1) The participating pupil will have achieved as much in the way of skills, abilities and understandings as he would have had he attended a monolingual school.	To determine if Spanish-speaking students participating in Coral Way learn as much as students who do not participate in the bilingual experiment. To compare learning between Spanish-speaking Coral Way students and Spanish-speaking students not attending Coral Way.	Content area tests (e.g. Stanford Achievement Test)
(2) He will be approximately as proficient in his second language (within his educational level) as he is in his first language.	To determine if both English- and Spanish-speaking students gain proficiency in a second language approximately equal to the first.	Language ability tests (e.g. Cooperative Inter-American Tests)

Notes

(1) Sánchez-Pando, J. (2008, March 13) Interview by R. Ruiz [audio file]. Coral Way Elementary. University of Florida Digital Collections. See http://ufdc.ufl.edu/ AA00065594/00001.

(2) See note 1.

(3) See note 1.

(4) See note 1.

(5) See note 1.

(6) Piñeiro, M. (2008, June 21) Interview by B. de Farber [audio file]. Coral Way Elementary. University of Florida Digital Collections. See https://ufdc.ufl.edu/ AA00065593/00001.

(7) Hall, J. (1961, October 6) Letter to A. Eurich (p. 51). Ford Foundation Archives. *The School Board of Dade County, Florida* (06300064). 17 December 1962 to 16 December 1965.

(8) Tierney, J. (1961, October 2) Memo to John B. Howard and Melvin J. Fox (p. 51). Ford Foundation Archives. *The School Board of Dade County, Florida* (06300064). 17 December 1962 to 16 December 1965.

(9) See note 8.

(10) Faust, C. (1962, November 1) Memo to H.T. Heald (p. 14). Ford Foundation Archives. *The School Board of Dade County, Florida* (06300064). 17 December 1962 to 16 December 1965.

(11) Hall, J. (1962, June 18) Letter to E.J. Meade, Jr. (p. 81). Ford Foundation Archives. *The School Board of Dade County, Florida* (06300064). 17 December 1962 to 16 December 1965.

(12) Mildenberger became director of the Division of College and University Assistance at the US Office of Education in 1962, shortly after his suggestion to Rojas to contact Ford. Mildenberger later led the founding of the American Council of Teacher of Foreign Languages (ACTFL) in 1966 (see Mildenberger, K.W., 'Prospects for a Unified Profession'. Speech to the National Federation of Modern Language Teachers Association, 1967).

(13) See note 8.

(14) N.A. (1961, November) Basic Program for Cuban Pupils (p. 129). Ford Foundation Archives. *The School Board of Dade County, Florida* (06300064). 17 December 1962 to 16 December 1965.

(15) See note 14.

(16) N.A. (N.D.) Grant Addendum: Outline of topics discussed at the meetings with the orientation teachers. 28–30 August and 1 September 1961 (p. 124). Ford Foundation Archives. *The School Board of Dade County, Florida* (06300064). 17 December 1962 to 16 December 1965.

(17) Hall, J. (1961, November 28) Letter to E.J. Meade, Jr. (p. 58). Ford Foundation Archives. *The School Board of Dade County, Florida* (06300064). 17 December 1962 to 16 December 1965.

(18) See note 17.

(19) Meade, E.J. (1962, January 17) Memo to A.C. Eurich. Subject: Dade County (Florida) Public Schools – Teaching English as a Second Language (p. 63). Ford Foundation Archives. *The School Board of Dade County, Florida* (06300064). 17 December 1962 to 16 December 1965.

(20) See note 19.

(21)   West, J. (1962, January 26) Revised grant proposal to Ford Foundation (p. 67). Ford Foundation Archives. *The School Board of Dade County, Florida* (06300064). 17 December 1962 to 16 December 1965.

(22)   The Colegio Americano de Guayaquil was opened by Harry and Mollie Jacobson in 1942 as a dual-language program with Ecuadorean and American children. I am not certain if this was the program that Rojas visited and referenced in her conceptualization of the Coral Way bilingual program.

(23)   See note 19.

(24)   Rojas had published the series with Fries (Rojas, P. and Fries, C. (1952) *Fries American English Series for the Study of English as a Second Language.* Boston, MA: D.C. Heath).

(25)   See note 19.

(26)   See note 6.

(27)   See note 1.

(28)   See note 1.

(29)   See note 1.

(30)   See note 1.

(31)   See note 14.

(32)   Board of Public Instruction of Dade County (1963, March 6). Excerpts from Minutes (p. 13). University of Florida Digital Collections. See https://ufdc.ufl.edu/AA00066056/00001.

(33)   See note 31.

(34)   Mann, P. (1965, December 16) Board caught in middle of parents' school battles (p. 37). *Miami Herald.*

(35)   Logan, J.L. (1963, April 14) Letter to all parents of first- and second-grade pupils. University of Florida Digital Collections. See https://ufdc.ufl.edu/AA00066047/00001.

(36)   Rojas, P. and Robinett, R. (1963, October 29) A report: Progress report on Ford Foundation Projects. University of Florida Digital Collections. See https://ufdc.ufl.edu/AA00066059/00001.

(37)   See note 1.

(38)   Logan, J.L. (1964–1967) Testing patterns for pupils in the bilingual school and the control groups. See https://ufdc.ufl.edu/AA00065851/00001.

(39)   Mann, P. (1967, October 4) The city with two tongues. La ciudad con dos lenguas (p. 14). *Miami Herald.*

References

Beckmann, G.M. (1964) The role of the foundations. *The Annals of the American Academy of Political and Social Science* 356, 12–22.

Bravo, E. (2010) *Operación Pedro Pan: A Documentary.* Bravo Films.

Carnoy, M., Gove, A.K. and Marshall, J.H. (2007) *Cuba's Academic Advantage: Why Students in Cuba Do Better in School.* Stanford, CA: Stanford University Press.

Cohen, L., Manion, L. and Morrison, K. (2011) *Research Methods in Education* (7th edn). New York: Routledge.

Conde, Y.M. (1999) *Operation Pedro Pan: The Untold Exodus of 14,048 Cuban Children.* New York: Routledge.

Dorner, L., Orellana, M.F. and Li-Grining, C.P. (2007) 'I helped my mom', and it helped me: Translating the skills of language brokers into improved standardized test scores. *American Journal of Education* 113 (3), 451–478.

Eire, C. (2004) *Waiting for Snow in Havana: Confessions of a Cuban Boy.* New York: Free Press.

Feinberg, R.C. (1999) Administration of two-way bilingual elementary schools: Building on strength. *Bilingual Research Journal* 23 (1), 47–68.

Gaardner, B.A. (1965) Teaching the bilingual child: Research, development, and policy. *The Modern Language Journal* 49 (3), 165–175.

García, O. (2009) *Bilingual Education in the 21st Century: A Global Perspective.* Malden, MA: John Wiley.

García, O. and Otheguy, R. (1985) The masters of survival send their children to school: Bilingual education in the ethnic schools of Miami. *The Bilingual Review/La Revista Bilingüe* 3–19.

Gonzalez-Pando, M. (2014) Polita Grau Pt. 2 of 2. *Cuban Living History Project of Florida International University, 1990–1997.* See https://libtube.fiu.edu/Play/276 (accessed 15 November 2018).

Grosjean, F. (1989) Neurolinguistics, beware! The bilingual is not two monolinguals in one person. *Brain and Language* 36 (1), 3–15. doi: 10.1016/0093-934x(89)90048-5

Guerra, L. (2012) *Visions of Power in Cuba: Revolution, Redemption, and Resistance, 1959–1971.* Chapel Hill, NC: University of North Carolina Press.

Inclán, R.G. (1972) Can bilingual-cultural education be the answer? *Educational Horizons* 50 (4), 192–196.

Inclán, R.G. (1979) The lessons from two decades of bilingual theory and practice of bilingual education. In J. Ornstein-Galicia and R. St. Clair (eds) *Bilingualism and Bilingual Education: New Readings and Insight* (pp. 3–15). San Antonio, TX: Trinity University.

Inclán, R.G. (1980) *A Report on the Cuban Students in Dade County Public Schools, Miami, Florida: Working Papers on Meeting the Education Needs of Cultural Minorities.* Education Commission of the States, Denver, CO.

Mackey, W.F. and Beebe, V.N. (1977) *Bilingual Schools for a Bicultural Community: Miami's Adaptation to the Cuban Refugees.* Rowley, MA: Newbury House.

Mitchell, W.L. (1962) The Cuban refugee program. *Social Security Bulletin* March, 3–8.

Ovando, C.J. (2003) Bilingual education in the United States: Historical development and current issues. *Bilingual Research Journal* 27 (1), 1–24.

Reyes, I., Kenner, C., Moll, L.C. and Orellana, M.F. (2012) Biliteracy among children and youths. *Reading Research Quarterly* 47 (3), 307–327.

Sandoval, M.C. (1991) Cultural contributions of the Cuban migrations into South Florida. In A. Jorge, J. Suchlicki and A.L. de Varona (eds) *Cuban Exiles in Florida: Their Presence and Contributions* (pp. 5–30). Research Institute for Cuban Studies, Miami, FL: North-South Center Publications.

Schiffman, H. (1987) Losing the battle for balanced bilingualism: The German-American case. *Language Problems and Language Planning* 11 (1), 66–81.

Stepick, A. and Stepick, C.D. (2009) Diverse contexts of reception and feelings of belonging. *Forum: Qualitative Social Research* 10 (3), Art 15.

Torres, M. (2003) *The Lost Apple: Operation Pedro Pan, Cuban Children in the U.S., and the Promise of a Better Future.* Boston, MA: Beacon Press.

Vidal de Haymes, M. (2004) Operation Pedro Pan: One family's journey to the U.S. *Journal of Poverty* 8 (4), 119–123.

2 The '50:50' Two-Way Model

In the Prologue and Chapter 1, I described the social and political context in which the Coral Way bilingual education program emerged following the political situation in Cuba. The unique combination of factors, namely the anticipated temporary stay of Cuban refugees following Castro's rise to power, the former social and economic Cuban ties to Florida, the large number of unaccompanied children who left Cuba under and outside of Operation Pedro Pan, all converged to create a sense of welcoming, generally speaking, for Cuban children and their families. In addition, the need to find a rapid solution for the education of Spanish-speaking children and the funding to do so also supported the establishment of Coral Way as a bilingual program and, later, a school. As the details of the program were established and implemented, positive sentiment toward the program as an instructional model grew. This chapter reviews the program and the way that educators in the early 1960s organized the program, students, teachers and aides.

The Instructional Model

Some of the earliest reports to the Ford Foundation on the progress of the grant-funded project noted the unique and experimental nature of the program, describing that the 'bilingual school represents a unique venture in American education. To our knowledge it is the only one of its kind to have been established so far'.[1] The sociopolitical climate was ripe for the establishment of bilingual education programs in the United States due to Cuban migration into Miami and migration trends worldwide. H.H. Stern describes a 1962 meeting held at the UNESCO Institute for Education in Hamburg, Germany, in which scholars across the world set a coherent research agenda related to establishing and examining foreign language education for young learners (Stern, 1969). Four years later, a second international convention of scholars was held, again in Hamburg, where scholars reported findings from their work. Among those reports was Paul Bell's (1969) paper on Coral Way Elementary. Worldwide, then, educators and scholars were examining bilingual education as a way to build linguistic resources, post-Sputnik.

In addition to a favorable national and international climate, the establishment of the Coral Way project in 1963 required additional factors and considerations, namely the correct number of English- and Spanish-speaking students who would participate in the 50:50 model; prepared personnel such as teaching staff and aides; and planning time in order to develop the curriculum and materials and to examine teaching methodologies. At the heart of these needs was the instructional model.

The model of instruction decided upon by Rojas, Bell and Robinett was theoretically 50:50, a ratio that refers both to the percentage of native speakers of each of the two languages and to the amount of instructional time spent in each language. For instance, 50% of the student participants needed to be native speakers of Spanish and 50% needed to be native speakers of English. Both groups of students would receive half of their instruction in English and half of their instruction in Spanish.

The original model was discussed and designed with a separation of native English and native Spanish speakers for instructional purposes. The original model did not mix or integrate native speakers of each language, and students were only integrated for a prescribed period of time in the middle of the school day. During that time, in the middle of the school day, native English-speaking and native Spanish-speaking children would interact for approximately one hour, depending on their grade level. No guidelines were specified for the language through which students should interact during the middle period of the day, and the aim was for this to be an unstructured and 'relaxed' time (Mackey & Beebe, 1977: 74). During this time, bilingual aides were responsible for engaging children in physical education (PE), lunch, supervised play and music and/or art.

The second and decidedly more important purpose of the midday hour was to allow the Spanish and English teachers time to co-plan their instruction each day. This was an essential and critical feature of the model, because teachers would switch rooms in the afternoon to instruct a different group of students, but they would primarily reinforce the content and concepts taught to students in the morning. The original plan directed that concepts would be 'taught in the native language in the morning, and then reinforced in the second language in the afternoon'.[2] Diana Morales, a graduate of Coral Way in the 1970s who began in fourth grade as a transfer student from New Jersey, described how 'students were double-dosed' in academic content.[3] These features allude to the proposed balanced instructional time (50:50) in both languages.

Instructional time

According to the proposed 50:50 model, students began the school day in their native language, referred to as the 'vernacular' in early school planning documents, and studied English language arts, mathematics, science, social studies and health.[4] They would then have an hour of PE, lunch, supervised play and music and/or art, all of which were supervised by Cuban aides, the first bilingual aides in the Dade County schools and in the early years of Coral Way. Cuban aides were Cuban women who were mostly trained in education in Cuba and who emigrated to the United States in the early 1960s. However, Cuban aides lacked the initial teacher credential in the United States, so they could not be hired as primary classroom instructors. They also had varying levels of English language ability.

Planning time for teachers

Planning time for teachers in the Coral Way experiment was essential to ensure that teachers were building on the curriculum across languages and not significantly repeating the curriculum. In the afternoon, students received instruction in the same subjects as the morning but through their second language. The last 10 or so minutes of each school day was reserved for 'student evaluation', where teachers would informally assess student learning and give short quizzes.

In reality, the 50:50 model was not that neatly rolled out. Coral Way began in 1963 with three grades (Grades 1, 2 and 3) simultaneously in Year 1 of implementation. First-grade students, however, did not have the same instructional time or curriculum as Grade 3 students. For example, in Weeks 1–4 of the school year, first graders had shortened school days, which allowed them to gradually adjust to a longer school day. Grade 1 students began the school year with 210 minutes of total instructional time in Weeks 1–4, followed by 330 instructional minutes in Weeks 5–24 and ending the school year with 390 instructional minutes in Weeks 25–36, the last trimester of school. The Coral Way model shifted the distribution of instructional time in each language for first-grade students, starting with 190 minutes of instruction in the vernacular in Weeks 1–4, and progressively reducing instructional time in the vernacular to 140 minutes in the final third of the school year (Weeks 13–36) (Table 2.1). Staff referred to the shifting distribution as 'staging'.

Table 2.1 Grade 1 schedule 1963

Weeks	Total time	Vernacular	Both languages	Second language	Second language distribution
1–4 incl.	210	190	0	20	Enrichment Songs, games
5–12 incl.	330	175	95*	60	Enrichment Systematic drill Arithmetic
13–24 incl.	330	140	95*	95	Enrichment Systematic drill Arithmetic Social studies Science, health, art
25–36 incl.	390	140	95*	155	Enrichment Systematic drill Arithmetic Social studies Science, health, reading, art

*Supervised play	20
Lunch	30
Physical education	30
Music	15
Total	95

Source: Reproduced from original.

Staging

Staging was the process of 'adding additional time to the classes taught in the second language until the student is spending about half of his day either in his second language class or in a mixed group'.[5] Staging was used for first-grade students as well as for second and third graders in Year 1 of the Coral Way experiment.

The organization of students in Grade 2 differed from that of Grade 1 students. In the case of beginning second-grade students, the total instructional time in school was 390 minutes each day throughout the school year. However, in Weeks 1–6 of the school year, students began instruction with 195 minutes in the vernacular, reduced to 165 minutes during Weeks 7–12. In the final trimester of the school year, the vernacular and second language were split evenly for instructional purposes (50:50) with 145 minutes each (Table 2.2).

The organization of Grade 3 students was similar to that of Grade 2. The total instructional time per day remained at 390 minutes, and there was also a gradual shift from more instruction in students' native language to more instruction in the second language. Third-grade students

Table 2.2 Grade 2 schedule 1963

Weeks	Total time	Vernacular	Both languages	Second language	Second language distribution
1–6 incl.	390	195	100*	95	Enrichment Systematic drill Arithmetic
7–12 incl.	390	165	100*	125	Enrichment Systematic drill Arithmetic Reading
13–36 incl.	390	145	100*	145	Enrichment Systematic drill Arithmetic Reading Social studies Science Health

*Supervised play	20
Lunch	20
Physical education	30
Music	20
Total	90

Source: Reproduced from original.

like second graders progressed toward a 50:50 balance across the two languages of instruction over the academic year (Table 2.3).

Later reports presented by Principal Logan in 1967 revealed that the actual instructional time in the second language for first graders was 15 minutes in Weeks 1–4, which was 5 minutes less than originally conceptualized in the original Ford Foundation proposal (Logan, 1967). The last grading period for first graders, Weeks 25–36, also changed from the original model to include more time in students' first language: 165 minutes, 75 minutes of mixed group (English and Spanish) and only 150 minutes of second language instruction. By the end of the initial three-year evaluation period for the Coral Way experiment, there was a notable change in instructional time by language for first-grade students (Table 2.1).

Separation of languages and students

What seems most evident from the foregoing instructional plans was the way that the administrators and teachers in the Coral Way experimental program separated languages and students following their belief

Table 2.3 Grade 3 schedule 1963

Weeks	Total time	Vernacular	Both languages	Second language	Second language distribution
1–6 incl.	390	195	100*	95	Enrichment Systematic drill Arithmetic
7–12 incl.	390	165	100*	125	Enrichment Systematic drill Arithmetic Reading
13–36 incl.	390	145	100*	145	Enrichment Systematic drill Arithmetic Reading Social studies Health
*Supervised play	20				
Lunch	30				
Physical education	30				
Music	20				
Total	90				

Source: Reproduced from original.

of primary language use in the home. The organization of students in 1963 was not predicated upon the social integration of students. If integration of students occurred, it was primarily an organic activity by virtue of the need for teacher planning time, which teachers and Principal Logan noted was an essential feature of the program, the structure of the school day and the use of Cuban aides – not actual teachers – to supervise children's play and lunchtime and to provide PE. Carol Shore, a student in the first-grade class in Coral Way who later transferred to a nearby English-only school, recalled her experience:

> I don't remember ever being with the Spanish-speaking group. I think we were totally segregated from them. I don't remember being with them at all, it just seemed like they just switched classes… when we would go to the Spanish classes, they would go to the English teachers, and we would go to the Spanish teachers.[6]

Students from the earliest classes of Coral Way noted similar separation. This was especially true among the English-speaking students who did not necessarily view the program as anything extraordinary, because they

interacted w... .... same language background for the majority of the school day, some only peripherally aware of the other.
Although in his 1963 and 1964 reports, Principal Logan noted the
'flexible organization plan'[7] of the program as one of the key aspects
leading to the program's overall success, this should not be confused
with the strict separation of languages used for instructional purposes.
The separation of languages and students, other than in the middle of the
school day, was a hallmark feature of the Coral Way bilingual program.
In addition to flexibility in organizing the instruction, Logan described
additional features of the program that led to its success: one hour a day
for essential planning time for teachers; the use of bilingual aides; 'democratic' planning in the school; and personnel and community enthusiasm
for the program. Logan felt that the daily planning time 'made the greatest contribution to the success of the bilingual program'.[8]

Identifying and placing students

In 1962, Coral Way was an English medium only school, meaning
that all students from kindergarten through Grade 6 received instruction
in English only. However, as noted earlier, the school neighborhood was
becoming more Spanish speaking and approaching a balance of students
speaking English and Spanish in their homes. Cuban aides were providing translation, interpretation and support for teachers and school staff,
but Dade County schools recognized that a different model, a better
program, could be created where students would benefit from instruction in two languages. Because the Cuban families felt that their time in
the United States was temporary, they had a strong desire to retain their
literacy in Spanish, to continue learning academic content and to acquire
English in order to communicate while living in the United States.

The demographics of the Coral Way neighborhood was mainly
English speaking before 1960–1961, but with a significant number of
school children who were Jewish and who attended a Hebrew heritage
language program on weekends, where they learned Hebrew.[9] Some children were in fact receiving multilingual language instruction: English,
Spanish and Hebrew. Identifying English speakers for the 1963 start of
the two-way program was not difficult. The difficulty was initiating the
program before there was a natural 50:50 balance between Spanish- and
English-speaking students.

Because Coral Way was a neighborhood school, Logan had to
assure parents who did not want their child to receive Spanish medium
instruction that different school accommodations could be arranged.

He emphasized to parents that 'participation was voluntary' and 'not limited to pupils with records of superior academic achievement'.[10] The school staff had anticipated that 80% of families, that is, the English-speaking families, would remain at Coral Way, and their estimate turned out to be correct.[11] The principal made arrangements for those students who wanted to relocate. A sample student transfer request by Principal Logan is shown in Figure 2.1.

As the program continued over the next few years, fewer numbers of students asked to be relocated to surrounding schools. Documents from 1964 indicate that only two students – one entering Grade 2 and one entering Grade 5 – transferred voluntarily to Silver Bluff Elementary School, an English-only program located about two miles from Coral Way. The following year, only one student requested a transfer. In 1966, however, the number of transfer requests was five students: two in Grade 3, two in Grade 4 and one in Grade 5. The number of transfer requests out of the Coral Way experimental program was surprisingly low, and Logan attributed students' ongoing participation in the program to parents seeing the linguistic and academic benefits of the program.[12]

On the other side of the 50:50 equation was identifying Spanish-speaking students for the experiment. The program needed

July 19, 1965

MEMORANDUM

To: Miss Lois Taylor, Director Elementary Education South Central District

From: _____. Principal Coral Way Elementary School J.L. Logan

Subject: TRANSFERRING OF TWO STUDENTS FROM CORAL WAY ELEMENTARY TO SILVER BLUFF ELEMENTARY FOR SCHOOL TERM 1965-1966

We have had a request from the parents of the following children to be transferred to Silver Bluff Elementary School as they do not wish their children to further participate in the bilingual programs:

James Corbly McCoun   Birthdate: 9/9/1958   Grade 2
Anne Porter McCoun   Birthdate: 5/18/1955   Grade 5

J.L. LOGAN
cc-Silver Bluff Elementary

Figure 2.1 Student transfer request by Principal Logan, 1965 (reproduced form original)

at least a close representation of Spanish speakers at 50% in order to balance the classrooms and teacher loads, which were planned for two classrooms at each grade level, from Grades 1 through 3. Initially, the program struggled to identify Spanish speakers in the Coral Way neighborhood, even though local families had been receiving children from the Pedro Pan Operation and Cuban families were moving into the community.

Logan noted that in the early stages, the district needed to broaden the neighborhood catchment:

> Inasmuch as the native Spanish speaking pupil in the school have been proportionately fewer than the native English speaking pupils, it has been necessary to open enrollment to Spanish speaking pupils from nearby Riverside and Shenandoah Elementary schools.[13]

Riverside and Shenandoah were each about 1.5 miles from Coral Way. Spanish-speaking students were initially relocated to Coral Way. However, by 1967–1968, demographic shifts to the Coral Way neighborhood tipped the percentage of Spanish-speaking students from 50% to 75% (Mackey & Beebe, 1977: 71). The result was unanticipated problems with the implementation of the program model.

Demographic and Instructional Changes

Two main problems impacted the smooth implementation of the experiment: the need to ensure and retain a relatively balanced 50:50 student population, and the need to group students according to their language ability levels in the second language.

First, as noted earlier, the neighborhood of Coral Way was selected, in part, because of its relatively balanced percentage of Spanish- and English-speaking students. Despite the fact that Operation Pedro Pan was no longer bringing unaccompanied children to the United States in 1963, Cuban families continued to move into the neighborhood. Tita Piñeiro assisted the school secretary with the registration of students for Coral Way between 1962 and 1964. As the program gained in popularity and more Spanish-speaking students arrived, the balance of students began to shift. Piñeiro explained to Principal Logan that they had 'enough kids now that we don't need to keep borrowing students from Southside'.[14] Principal Logan, deeply committed to the program and to the Spanish-speaking students' academics and welfare, responded, 'No, those parents let us have them here, so we have to open another bilingual room in each grade level'.[15]

The second problem emerged because new students were continually enrolling in the community school without having had prior bilingual education schooling and had low levels of literacy in Spanish or English. In other words, transfer students, especially those whose last names sounded 'Latino', came from English-only schools and without literacy in Spanish.

In addition, not all incoming students were entering Coral Way beginning in kindergarten or Grade 1. The issue of transfer students, whether from prior US elementary schools where students learned to read and write in English, or incoming students from Cuba who learned to read and write in Spanish, challenged the 'balanced bilingualism' goal, because those students could not keep up with their grade-level peers in reading and writing. This caused disruption in placing students in the correct 'vernacular' classroom for the first half of the day and in teaching the curriculum, which had to be aligned daily and weekly, in order for teachers to repeat and extend it to second language learners in the afternoon. Logan's solution to the transfer 'problem' was to assign students to small groups for part of the school day each day in order to learn 'basic language patterns'.[16] Thus, small groups of Spanish as a second language (SSL) or English as a second language (ESL) students were pulled out of their regular classroom placement and focused on language development.

In a report prepared in mid-1964, Logan also indicated that there was an overall increase in the number of students to Coral Way. Rather than increasing the number of students in the existing classrooms, mainly first and second grades that had a total of four teachers, two in Spanish (Cuban aides trained as teachers) and two in English with former English-only teachers, new classes were added that did not follow the model of teachers switching classrooms to provide content instruction through their native language. In late 1964, Logan described 'with one exception, the basic overall organization of the school today is the same as the original plan. However, because of an increased enrollment, two rooms, one at first and one at second grade level, have been set up as self contained classes'. Students remained with one teacher for the entire school day, described as a 'bilingual teacher', who provided instruction in Spanish and English, switching mid-day to the second language.[17]

Assessment of Languages

Few assessments of language were available in 1963, and the school had no systematic way to determine students' abilities in Spanish or English. Mabel Richardson proposed to study students' learning as part of her doctoral dissertation work at the University of Miami. However, unlike today's educational environment, there was no quick assessment 'screener' of students' language ability levels, nor was there a home language survey, widely used in today's schools, to ask parents about the actual language use of students in the home. Teachers and administrators relied on their intuition, interpretation and informal 'bilingual interviews' with the children.[18]

Former students such as Bess de Farber and Orestes Gonzalez recalled not knowing who was selected for which group, English or Spanish, because many of the students had 'Spanish-sounding last names'[19] but were placed in English-speaking classes. In other words, no systematic language assessment was conducted with new incoming students to determine their 'vernacular' or their placement in the program. This caused much disruption in the early model.

As a result of the lack of assessments and difficulty in determining the students' language abilities English and Spanish, a significant amount of re-arranging of students took place in 1963. Logan referred to this as the program having flexible scheduling; however, in reality, 'the first year there was a great deal of shifting of pupils from one group to another'.[20]

Thus, identifying the appropriate placement for students was neither systematic nor based on any standardized assessments. Orestes Gonzalez, a student who started school at Coral Way and graduated from the first class in 1968, recalls that the students were grouped based loosely on their language ability levels as determined by teacher judgment and observation:

> I remember feeling a sense of relief that I wasn't put into that third group. There was an elite group [group 1], mostly American kids, English-speaking kids. I was in the second group, kids that were totally balanced in English and Spanish. And then there was the third group. I remember they were mostly Spanish speakers, kids that had recently arrived from Cuba, or had not been fully integrated into what was going on in Coral Way at that moment, only because they were recent arrivals.[21]

Gladys Margarita Diaz provides another example. She and her mother arrived from Cuba in March 1962, and were relocated from Miami to Mountain View, California, where a family 'adopted' them. She began summer school in California in 1962. Her father, who had been an electrical engineer in Cuba and who was determined to be a security risk by the Castro government, ended up working in a box factory in Cuba and later left for Spain.

Upon learning that other relatives had left Cuba and were then living in Miami, Gladys Margarita and her mother returned to the Miami area and found themselves living five blocks from Coral Way Elementary. Able to speak 'perfect English' due to the intensive summer school experience, Gladys Margarita was immediately placed into the English class in the bilingual program:

> When I got interviewed, I was put with the English native speaker group. And my cousin, who had arrived from Cuba in August, was put with the Spanish-speaking group. So that was like a major crisis for us, because we were very close, almost like brother and sister.[22]

Teachers in the program were astounded by Gladys Margarita's oral English ability and called her mother on the phone stating, 'your child is a prodigy; she speaks perfect English'. Her mother countered that her daughter had been in a summer all-English program in California. Teachers soon realized, however, that Gladys Margarita could not read or write in English. Gonzalez experienced a similar shift:

> I was either five and a half or six years old at that time, and they put me in with the Spanish speakers first. And after four or five weeks, or maybe it was less, they assigned me to the English-speaking group, because they saw that I had a natural ability to acquire the English language pretty quickly.[23]

In Gonzalez's case, the increase in the number of Spanish speakers warranted students being quickly regrouped into the English classes, once they had attained some level of English ability. Determining students' placements was based primarily on students' oral language ability, and secondarily on the ratio of English- and Spanish-speaking students.

Student Report Cards

Bessie de Farber entered Coral Way in first grade in 1962 when Coral Way was an English-only school. Bess, her parents and younger brother moved into the neighborhood more by chance than by planning. Her family was offered the opportunity to rent a home that was directly across the street from the Coral Way school. As a practicing Jewish family, the neighborhood's synagogue, Beth David, offered an opportunity for the children to attend twice-weekly Hebrew classes. Bess was one of the Coral Way students who experienced multilingual education, because of her participation in Beth David and Coral Way.

A comparison of Bess's report cards demonstrates not only how schools assessed student learning in the 1960s, but also, and importantly, how the Coral Way experiment, which changed educational program models between 1962–1963 and 1963–1964, was reflected in how students were assessed. In 1962 and 1963, there were six grading periods for students, which were each six weeks long. Both years included student attendance, student date of birth and the student's main teacher. The report cards also indicated student 'progress in habits and attitudes' such as cooperation and courtesy, including respect for authority and thoughtfulness, study habits, personal appearance and respect for property (Figures 2.2 and 2.3).[24]

However, changes to the Coral Way academic program warranted changes in student assessment and reporting. In 1963–1964, for example, Bess's second-grade report card shows her first language teacher, Mrs Heydrick, and her second language teacher, Mrs Gonzalez. Bess's morning classes or 'vernacular' were conducted in English and her afternoon, second language classes, were in Spanish with Mrs Gonzalez.[25] Although Bess's mother tongue was Spanish, and Spanish was used as the primary language of communication in her home, Bess was assigned to the English-speaking

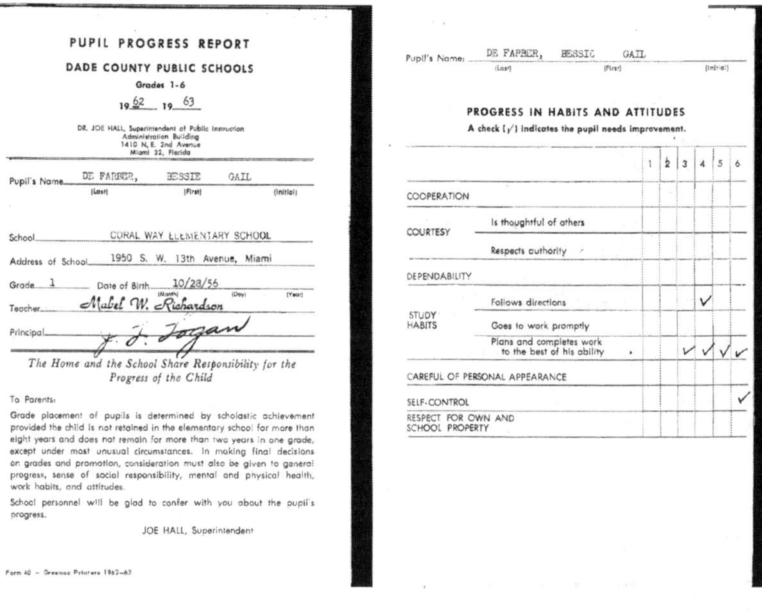

Figure 2.2 Bess de Farber first-grade report card, 1962–1963, pp. 1–2 (original)

PUPIL PROGRESS REPORT

CORAL WAY BILINGUAL ELEMENTARY SCHOOL
1950 S. W. Thirteenth Avenue

19_63___ 19_64__
DADE COUNTY PUBLIC SCHOOLS
DR. JOE HALL, Superintendent of Public Instruction
Administration Building
1410 N.E. 2nd Avenue
Miami 32, Florida

Pupil's Name___DE FARBER_____BESSIE_____G.___
                (Last)   (First)   (Initial)

Grade___TWO___ Date of Birth___Oct.___ 28___ 56___
                                (Month) (Day) (Year)

First Language Teacher___MRS. MARGARET HEYDRICK_____

Second Language Teacher___MRS. JULIETA GONZALEZ____

Principal___J. J. Fitzgerald___

*The Home and the School Share Responsibility for the
Progress of the Child*

To Parents:
Grade placement of pupils is determined by scholastic achievement
provided the child is not retained in the elementary school for more than
eight years and does not remain for more than two years in one grade,
except under most unusual circumstances. In making final decisions
on grades and promotion, consideration must also be given to general
progress, sense of social responsibility, mental and physical health,
work habits, and attitudes.
School personnel will be glad to confer with you about the pupil's
progress.
                        JOE HALL, Superintendent

Pupil's Name:___DE FARBER_____BESSIE_____G.___
                 (Last)   (First)   (Initial)

PROGRESS IN HABITS AND ATTITUDES
A check (✓) indicates the pupil needs improvement.

	1	2	3	4	5	6
COOPERATION						
COURTESY — Is thoughtful of others						
— Respects authority						
DEPENDABILITY						
STUDY HABITS — Follows directions						
— Goes to work promptly		✓			✓	
— Plans and completes work to the best of his ability						
CAREFUL OF PERSONAL APPEARANCE						
SELF-CONTROL						
RESPECT FOR OWN AND SCHOOL PROPERTY						

ATTENDANCE

Days Present	28	29	29	30	28	30
Days Absent	2	0	2	0	2	0
Times Tardy	0	0	0	0	0	0

Figure 2.3 Bess de Farber second-grade report card, 1963–1964, pp. 1–2 (original)

teacher in the morning. She suspects that this was because her English was very good, having completed all of first grade in English.[26]

A comparison of pages 3 and 4 of Bess de Farber's report cards from 1962–1963 and 1963–1964 demonstrates changes in the academic content areas for Coral Way.

In 1962–1963, Bess's report cards included all of the traditional school subjects then taught at Coral Way (see Figure 2.4). Her first-grade teacher was Mabel Richardson, the same educator who later completed a doctorate degree at the University of Miami and who conducted the only known study of Coral Way's students using a standardized test in her 1968 dissertation. The first-grade English-only subjects that were assessed on the report card included English language arts (listed in the order of reading, English, spelling and writing), social studies, health, PE, arithmetic, science, art, music and 'conversational Spanish'.[27]

By 1963–1964, the subjects assessed on student report cards changed to include 'First Language' followed by an underline to indicate which was the first language, in the order of reading, oral and written language, spelling and writing. Underneath the First Language section was the Second Language section, also underlined to indicate the second language of

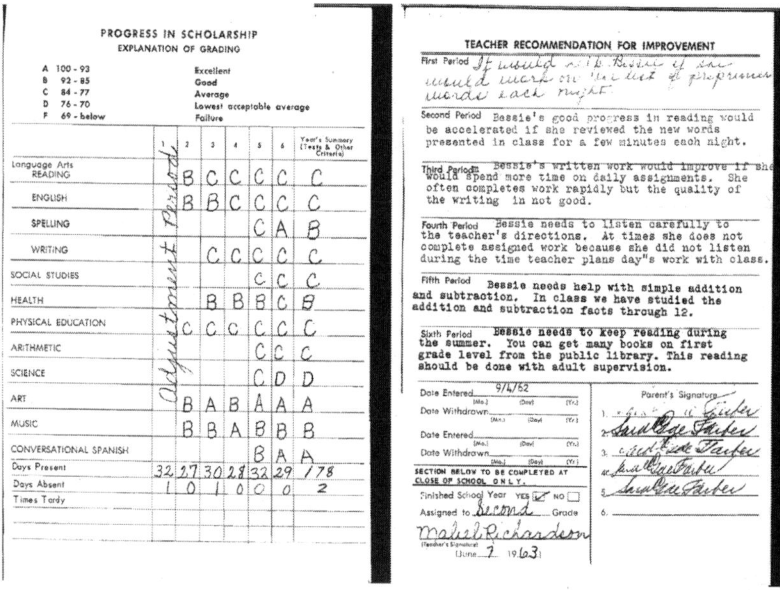

PROGRESS IN SCHOLARSHIP
EXPLANATION OF GRADING

A 100 - 93 Excellent
B 92 - 85 Good
C 84 - 77 Average
D 76 - 70 Lowest acceptable average
F 69 - below Failure

	1	2	3	4	5	6	Year's Summary (Tests & Other Criteria)
Language Arts READING	Adjustment Period	B	C	C	C	C	C
ENGLISH		B	B	C	C	C	C
SPELLING					C	A	B
WRITING			C	C	C	C	C
SOCIAL STUDIES					C	C	C
HEALTH			B	B	B	C	B
PHYSICAL EDUCATION		C	C	C	C	C	C
ARITHMETIC					C	C	C
SCIENCE					C	D	D
ART		B	A	B	A	A	A
MUSIC		B	B	A	B	B	B
CONVERSATIONAL SPANISH					B	A	A
Days Present	32	27	30	28	32	29	178
Days Absent	1	0	1	0	0	0	2
Times Tardy							

TEACHER RECOMMENDATION FOR IMPROVEMENT

First Period It would [illegible] Bessie if she would work on the list of preprimer words each night.

Second Period Bessie's good progress in reading would be accelerated if she reviewed the new words presented in class for a few minutes each night.

Third Period Bessie's written work would improve if she would spend more time on daily assignments. She often completes work rapidly but the quality of the writing in not good.

Fourth Period Bessie needs to listen carefully to the teacher's directions. At times she does not complete assigned work because she did not listen during the time teacher plans day"s work with class.

Fifth Period Bessie needs help with simple addition and subtraction. In class we have studied the addition and subtraction facts through 12.

Sixth Period Bessie needs to keep reading during the summer. You can get many books on first grade level from the public library. This reading should be done with adult supervision.

Date Entered 9/4/62 (Mo.) (Day) (Yr.)
Date Withdrawn (Mo.) (Day) (Yr.)
Date Entered (Mo.) (Day) (Yr.)
Date Withdrawn (Mo.) (Day) (Yr.)

SECTION BELOW TO BE COMPLETED AT CLOSE OF SCHOOL ONLY.
Finished School Year YES ✓ NO
Assigned to Second Grade
Mabel Richardson
(Teacher's Signature)
June 7 1963

Parent's Signature
1.
2.
3.
4.
5.
6.

Figure 2.4 Bess de Farber first-grade report card, 1962–1963, pp. 3–4 (original)

the student. Recall that for Bess, her first, home language was actually Spanish. The order of second language assessment was 'aural comprehension' or listening, speaking, reading, written composition and 'Application in Subject Areas'. The report card suggests that students' listening skills in the second language preceded their speaking skills, and those were followed by literacy development, namely reading and writing, and then application to school content areas (see Figure 2.5).

Teachers at Coral Way, along with the Cuban aides, Principal Logan and staff were very serious about and focused on ensuring that both groups of students developed high levels of literacy in both languages. This meant that English literacy was emphasized for the Spanish-speaking students and Spanish literacy was emphasized for the English-speaking students. Carol Shore was a first-grade student in Coral Way in 1963–1964. She recalled her parents knowing little about the program at Coral Way and not enjoying the second half of her school day, which took place in Spanish. She recalled:

> I did not like going to Spanish three hours a day. I know I didn't like it. I loved going to school for the English program, but not for the Spanish. You know, we didn't speak Spanish in my home, and I didn't feel like I

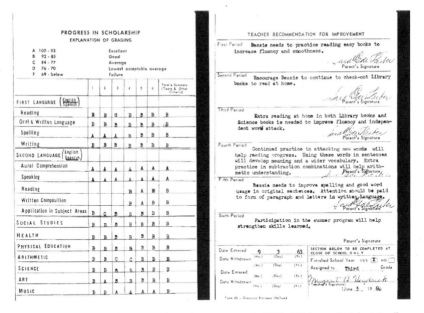

Figure 2.5 Bess de Farber second-grade report card, 1963–1964, pp. 3–4 (original)

really understood it, and I know I didn't do well in it. I don't think it was good for my self-esteem to start school, receiving 'D's' and 'F's' on my report card in a language that I was not brought up to speak.[28]

Carol's report card demonstrates the difficulties that Carol faced in Spanish. It also shows the intense and serious insistence of the Spanish teachers on English-speaking students' learning of Spanish language and literacy (Figure 2.6).

Teachers were uncompromising. First, they faced public scrutiny in ensuring that the program was implemented with fidelity during its first year. Second, they knew that this was an experiment never conducted before and the school district would need assurances that students were learning and using both languages orally and in writing.

The two-way immersion model of bilingual education was predicated upon both a fairly even number of students who were native Spanish speaking and native English speaking, as well as a model of bilingual education that was theoretically and soundly based on students' ability to transfer their learning across languages. What occurred in the early years of the model was that it was not strictly a 50:50 model of instructional time. The program also struggled to maintain a 50:50

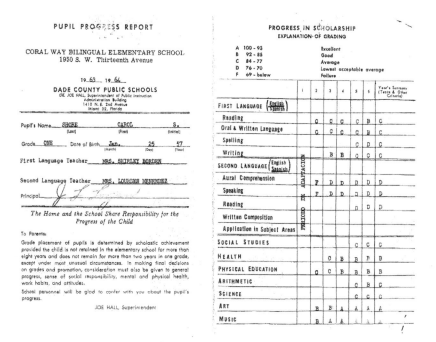

Figure 2.6 Carol Shore's report card, 1963–1964, pp. 1 and 3 (original)

balance in the number of students across both groups, as the number of Spanish-speaking students continued to arrive into the area. There was a strict separation of language for instructional purposes during the mornings and afternoons in the core academic subjects, but during the mid-day non-academic subjects (e.g. art and PE), students had no language use restrictions.

Phases II and III of the Model

In subsequent years of Coral Way, namely between 1964 and 1967, two additional changes were made to the instructional model. Mackey and Beebe (1977) describe three distinct organizational phases. The first organizational phase used grade-level groupings according to students' first language. Described at the beginning of this chapter, this initial model was based on the assumption that students who could read well in their first language could communicate and read equally well in the second language. However, as noted in this chapter, the transfer of students from different (English only) schools into Coral Way, along with the change in demographics and increasing numbers of Spanish speakers in the Coral Way neighborhood proved this assumption inaccurate. As a result, a second organizational phase was considered and implemented.

In the second organizational phase, students were grouped by first language based on their reading ability level for morning instruction. However, in the afternoon, students were regrouped, irrespective of their grade level, according to their oral language ability in the second language. Mackey and Beebe note three language ability levels used at Coral Way during the 1966–1967 school year:

a. *Independent pupils*, who had high oral language ability in the second language
b. *Intermediate pupils*, who required more assistance but who understood most of the instruction;
c. *Non-independent pupils*, who required significant scaffolding, or instructional support, to communicate and use the language. (Mackey & Beebe, 1977: 74)

Readers will recall that those levels were actually established in the early Dade County Public Schools (DCPS) orientation teacher plan for Cuban refugee children in 1961 by Dr Pauline Rojas. Teachers began to realize almost immediately that a major strength of the program, the ability of the English and Spanish teachers to co-plan during the school day, was hindered by the differentiated student groupings. This was because students were transferring in and across grade levels for instructional purposes (Table 2.4).

As seen in Table 2.4, between 1963 when the model was proposed and 1967 when Logan gave a report on the implementation of the model, changes were made to the actual amount of time through which students were instructed in each language. For instance, from 1963 to 1967, a first-grade student received 25 additional minutes of instructional time in his or her first language, while instructional time in the second language was reduced by 5 minutes per day, and the time for enrichment activities

Table 2.4 1963 versus 1967 language use for Grade 1 students (Weeks 24–36)

Grade 1 students Weeks 24–36 (final trimester)	1963 proposal	1967 report
Total time	390	390
Vernacular (native language instruction)	140 (36%)	165 (42%)
Both languages (PE, lunch, supervised play)	95 (24%)	75 (19%)
Second language instruction	155 (40%)	150 (38%)

was reduced by 20 minutes. The shift in the instructional time likely reflected teacher input into the development of literacy for first graders and spoke to the need for children in the early grades to have additional instructional time and support in the first language.

A third organizational phase was established in the late 1960s, namely between 1967 and 1968 and later at Coral Way, which consisted of a combination of the Phase I structure and the Phase II organizational structure. Students were grouped by native language reading ability in the morning using high, average and low ability groupings. In the afternoon, students' oral language ability in the second language determined their classes but only *within* grade levels. Thus, students would still switch between the two languages for instructional purposes, but their classes (referred to as groupings) were based on language ability – specifically, students' reading ability in the first language and students' oral language ability in the second language. Afternoons continued to provide 'reinforcement, enrichment, and extension' of the morning curriculum (Mackey & Beebe, 1977: 75).

As this chapter has shown, the bilingual program at Coral Way was neither rigid nor stable. Coral Way staff and teachers originally aimed for a 50:50 ratio of students and a sliding distribution of language use as a medium of instruction right from the beginning of the plan (staging). However, changes in demographics toward an increasing number of Spanish-speaking students, as well as the issue of students transferring into Coral Way Elementary required changes to the model within the first two years of its implementation.

The model was changed first to accommodate transfer students through a pull-out second language support structure. Second, to accommodate new students, two self-contained Grade 1 and Grade 2 classrooms were added where teachers did not switch classrooms; students had only one teacher. Third, the model was changed to more accurately respond to students' ability levels in reading and writing the languages, something that was not conducted at the initial implementation, when teachers relied on oral interviews with students for their placement in to the correct vernacular home room (Phase II). This posed problems with students crossing grade levels and teachers therefore not having adequate, daily co-planning time. Finally, in the third phase of the model, students were regrouped within grade levels for language support. The last phase of the model, which occurred in the 1967–1968 school year, re-established co-planning time for teachers.

The Coral Way bilingual program evolved from an idea by Dr Pauline Rojas and her immediate staff members Ralph Robinett, Paul Bell,

J. Lee Logan and numerous teacher-educators and teachers whose commitment to bilingual development was supported by their belief in the program's long-term social and cultural benefits to society. This chapter has described the program model, the variations in the program model, the problems faced by teachers and the difficulty in the early years of the program in determining some of the students' home language. The model was predicated upon strict language separation to learn academic content, but its flexibility to reassign students based on their language learning needs and the design of the program that ensured co-planning time for teachers were strengths noted by its early leaders.

Notes

(1) Rojas, P. and Robinett, R. (1963, October 29) A report: Progress report on Ford Foundation Projects. University of Florida Digital Collections. See https://ufdc.ufl.edu/AA00066059/00001.
(2) Richardson, M.W. (1964, May 14) A study of certain aspects of the achievement of Coral Way Elementary pupils in the bilingual program. Unpublished project proposal. University of Florida Digital Collections. See https://ufdc.ufl.edu/AA00066042/00001.
(3) Morales, D. (2018, October 13). Interview by M. R. Coady [Audio file]. Coral Way Elementary. University of Florida Digital Collections.
(4) Coral Way Sample Daily Schedule (1963) University of Florida Digital Collections. See https://ufdc.ufl.edu/AA00065987/00001.
(5) Loveland, C.L. (1966, December 9) Coral Way Elementary: A Bilingual School. University of Florida Digital Collections. See https://ufdc.ufl.edu/AA00066052/00001.
(6) Shore, C. (2008, July 10) Interview by B. de Farber [audio file]. Coral Way Elementary. University of Florida Digital Collections. See https://ufdc.ufl.edu/AA00065598/00001.
(7) Logan, J.L. (c. 1964) Coral Way: A Bilingual School Speech. University of Florida Digital Collections. See https://ufdc.ufl.edu/AA00066053/00001.
(8) See note 6.
(9) de Farber, B. (2019) Interview by M.R. Coady [audio file]. Coral Way Elementary. University of Florida Digital Collections and Shore, C.K. (2008, July 10) Interview by B. de Farber [audio file]. Coral Way Elementary. University of Florida Digital Collections. See https://ufdc.ufl.edu/AA00065598/00001.
(10) See note 6.
(11) See note 1.
(12) See note 6.
(13) See note 1, p. 5.
(14) Piñeiro, M. (2008, June 21) Interview by B. de Farber [audio file]. Coral Way Elementary. University of Florida Digital Collections. See https://ufdc.ufl.edu/AA00065593/00001.
(15) See note 13.
(16) See note 6, p. 8.
(17) See note 6, p. 8.
(18) Sánchez-Pando, J. (2008, March 13) Interview by R. Ruiz [audio file]. Coral Way Elementary. University of Florida Digital Collections. See http://ufdc.ufl.edu/AA00065594/00001.

(19) Gonzalez, O. (2008, March 26) Interview by R. Ruiz [audio file]. Coral Way Elementary. University of Florida Digital Collections. See https://ufdc.ufl.edu/AA00065599/00001.
(20) See note 6, p. 5.
(21) See note 18.
(22) Diaz, G.M. and Diaz, J.G. (2008, March 15) Interview by R. Ruiz [audio file]. Coral Way Elementary. University of Florida Digital Collections. See https://ufdc:ufl.edu/AA00065600/00001.
(23) See note 18.
(24) de Farber, B. (1963, June 7) Pupil Progress Report: Dade County Public Schools. Coral Way Elementary. University of Florida Digital Collections. See https://ufdc.ufl.edu/AA00066024/00001.
(25) See note 23.
(26) de Farber, B. (2008, March 11) Interview by R. Ruiz [audio file]. Coral Way Elementary. University of Florida Digital Collections. See https://ufdc.ufl.edu/AA00065601/00001.
(27) See note 25.
(28) See note 5.

References

Bell, P.W. (1969) Bilingual education in an American elementary school. In H.H. Stern (ed.) *Languages and the Young School Child* (pp. 112–118). London: Oxford University Press.
Logan, J.T. (1967) Coral Way: A bilingual school. *TESOL Quarterly* 1 (2), 50–54.
Mackey, W.F. and Beebe, V.N. (1977) *Bilingual Schools for a Bicultural Community: Miami's Adaptation to the Cuban Refugees*. Rowley, MA: Newbury House.
Stern, H.H. (1969) Introduction. In H.H. Stern (ed.) *Languages and the Young School Child* (pp. 3–8). London: Oxford University Press.

3 Cuban Educators: Aides, 'The Marines' and Teachers

In Chapters 1 and 2, I described the social and political context of the earliest two-way immersion Coral Way bilingual program and the vision and implementation of the model. The success or failure of the Coral Way bilingual program could not be determined academically without student learning outcomes in both Spanish and English. However, to achieve the goal of ensuring positive outcomes and high-quality instruction, one of the most important resources needed for the experiment was the preparation of teachers to work with both sets of children – Spanish and English speakers – across different content areas in the elementary classroom. One of Logan's earliest tasks as program and school principal was to ensure that he had the correct number of teachers. Dade County schools dictated that all teachers should be native speakers of the languages that they taught. In other words, only native Spanish-speaking teachers would teach in Spanish, and only native English-speaking teachers would teach in English.

At the beginning of Year 1 of the experiment, in collaboration with the Dade County district-level team, Logan aimed to begin the 1963 school year with two classes of Spanish-speaking and English-speaking first grades (four classes), two classes of Spanish-speaking and English-speaking second grades (four classes) and two classes of Spanish-speaking and English-speaking third grades (four classes; a total of 12 classrooms with six native Spanish-speaking teachers and six native English-speaking teachers. The total number of participating students was about 360.[1]

In addition to their ability in their native language and having a high degree of literacy in the language, the teachers in the bilingual program also needed to have a high degree of content area knowledge in mathematics, science, social studies, health and language arts, as well as the ability to teach that academic content. Essentially, the teachers needed the following skills: (1) knowledge of language, English or Spanish, and how that language worked; (2) knowledge of teaching the language as a second language; (3) knowledge of academic content; and (4) knowledge of how to teach academic content to children through their second language.

Along with the large number of Cuban children arriving in Miami from 1960 to 1962 were teachers and professors educated in languages and pedagogy in Cuba. Some of the teachers who arrived in Miami in the early 1960s had been teachers of the English language or had been trained as teachers for Cuban children. These educators became a pillar of the experimental bilingual program, first as Cuban aides, then in preparation as teachers and self-described as 'The Marines', and later as fully credentialed Florida teachers in the bilingual program.

'Cuban Aides'

Before Coral Way was designated a bilingual education experiment in 1963, former Cuban teachers had been working across Dade County schools to assist existing teachers with the influx of Cuban children. Data from Dade County estimate that between 1959 and 1962 about 200,000 Cubans left Cuba for the United States, and that there were about 20,000 new Spanish-speaking students in Miami schools (Pérez, 1986; Way & Haden, 1966).

Tita Piñeiro began working at Coral Way in October 1961. She had been in the United States for about a year when she applied for a job at the school. Piñeiro's work as a Cuban aide was to assist the teachers in clerical tasks, translate and interpret when needed and supervise the children during the middle of the school day. She applied to Coral Way because she had heard that the school needed bilinguals to assist English-speaking teachers with Cuban children.

Josefina Sánchez, who was one of the first Cuban aides and a credentialed teacher in Cuba, describes the scene prior to Coral Way establishing the bilingual program as 'berserk, because for a school district to absorb, in a year and a half [thousands of students], you need desks, rooms to put those desks in. You needed a teacher for that room. You needed books, which were nonexistent, books, which they could not read. How could they get along in that classroom?'.[2]

The urgent need for bilingual staff was quickly evident in Dade County. As a support provision, the district hired former Cuban teachers to work as Cuban aides. Sánchez described the aide as 'a teacher from Cuba who could speak English – [for] better or worse – but could make herself or himself understood – who was placed in a room with an American teacher, with a bunch of American children, and here was this angel person who came – because they weren't teachers, they were angels'.

The Ford Foundation-funded Cuban retraining program enabled the Cuban aides to train for a Florida teacher credential. However, at the time, despite the fact that many teachers had experience and were bilingual and some had been professors at the University of Havana, they had no status in the United States. Piñeiro was the second Cuban aide hired by Coral Way and worked at the school between 1961 and 1970. Despite the low wage of $18 a day, Piñeiro found it 'a great experience. Half of the day I was working in the office, at the counter, doing registration'. But the work was challenging for the staff, who described needing patience and understanding due to the pressures. Piñeiro was physically exhausted and found the work difficult.[3]

Cuban aides' schedule

Cuban aides were assigned to clerical duties and non-instructional work in the early days of the experiment. During the first year of the Coral Way experiment, three Cuban aides were hired, the only additional school personnel allowed by the district. The Cuban aides were the only 'overstaffing' of the school, that is, additional personnel costs used to support the bilingual program (Bell, 1969: 115). While they assisted teachers in classrooms, they were not responsible for delivering any academic content in mathematics, science, social studies, health or language arts. Gonzalez recalls that aides provided classes outside of the aforementioned core subjects:

> I do know that we would always look forward to the art classes. One of the aides would come in, pushing her cart full of art supplies and equipment, and we'd spend a couple of hours. I don't know if it was once every two weeks or once a month, but that was something we would always look forward to.[4]

Table 3.1 shows a sample of the daily schedule for Cuban aide 2, demonstrating the Cuban aides' scope of work.[5] Their work included clerical duties such as taking student attendance, supervising students on the playground and in the corridor, instructing art and physical education and supervising lunchtime. They were also required to type the student report cards, which had to be different for Coral Way students to reflect the two languages.[6] Report cards were sent home six times a year.

Table 3.1 Cuban aide 2 schedule (1963–1964)

Time	Minutes	
8:15–8:30	15	Supervise second-grade corridor
8:30–9:05	35	Clerical duties (pupil accounting routine)
9:05–9:35	20	Planning
9:35–9:55	20	Supervised play (Grade 1)
9:55–10:15	20	Supervised play (Grade 2)
10:15–10:35	20	Supervised play (Grade 3)
10:35–10:55	20	Art (Grade 2) Monday and Tuesday – Team II English Wednesday and Thursday – Team II English
11:00–12:00	60	Lunchroom supervision
12:00–12:30	30	Lunch
12:30–1:00	30	Physical education (Grade 1 – Team I)
1:00–1:30	30	Physical education (Grade 1 – Team II)
1:30–2:00	30	Physical education (Grade 2 – Team I)
2:00–2:30	30	Physical education (Grade 2 – Team II)
2:30–2:50	20	Art (Grade 3) Monday and Tuesday – Team II English Wednesday and Thursday – Team II Spanish Friday – clerical duties

Source: Reproduced from original.

Sánchez describes what happened in 1962 when Cuban children continued to register in Dade County schools. 'Cuban aides became "teachers" in quotations', she notes, 'because they were no longer serving Mrs. Smith in her room, translating for the kids, pulling them to a little group, interpreting for them what was going on, teaching them in Spanish what the teacher was saying in English, giving them some sort of background.... If they were talking about the stars and the planets, they had the vehicle, there was no language to communicate what was going on'.[7] The Cuban aides' work was essential to the initial and ongoing functioning of the bilingual program. Their time with students allowed the teachers non-instructional time to engage in planning and curriculum development, an essential component in the Coral Way experiment.

'The Marines'

Once Coral Way had been named as the experimental site in spring 1963, Robinett, Rojas and Logan worked together to detail the implementation of the program and the two main goals related to instruction: to prepare teachers for Spanish-speaking children and to create materials for teachers and students to use in the experimental program. At the time, both Dade County schools and the Ford Foundation agreed that one of the highest priorities was the need for highly qualified teachers to work with Cuban refugee children. As noted in Chapter 1, funding for the program targeted teacher education. The Ford Foundation funded the project in part based on the objective of Dade County to create materials that could be used across the United States, as the demand nationally among school districts for English as a second language (ESL) materials burgeoned.

Cuban teacher retraining program

The University of Miami (UM) initiated the first class to prepare Cuban refugee teachers to teach Spanish in Florida schools. Some had already been working as Cuban aides in Dade County but lacked a Florida teaching credential. The state of Florida agreed to grant three-year provisional teaching certificates to the first group of teachers to obtain the teaching credential through the UM program, called the Cuban Teacher Retraining Program. Up to 30 participants were invited to apply to the first group of teachers in the teacher credential program, and they were selected based on a competitive application process. However, 33 scored high enough to gain entrance, and all were allowed to enroll.

Sánchez recalled that the 'Ford Foundation only placed money for thirty people. And when everybody took their tests and all the papers were clear... there were three persons at the end of the line [beyond] the thirtieth position that had everything the same. So they called and said, "What do we do? How do we break the tie? Alphabetically?", And Ford Foundation said, "No, take the other three". So we were thirty-three Marines'.[7]

Although the group referred to themselves as the Marines at the university, the *double entendre* of the word 'marines' can be interpreted two ways: as ruthless warriors who blazed a trail for others to follow, or possibly as a cultural reference of nationalist sentiment toward the United States. In either case, the group's self-label demonstrates a show of force by the earliest Cuban aides who fought for the teaching credential and the possibility to teach in Florida. The job of these marines was extremely difficult, and they faced language and cultural discrimination in the teacher retraining program. Sánchez could not emphasize enough the challenges. Her voice rises loudly as her fist hits the table, 'we had a very rough time at the University of Miami: the *roughest*, the *meanest*, the most *denigrating* time that anybody... those first two groups of teachers... we sweated it out, we were Marines. Our corps paved the way for all the rest of the teachers of all the programs of all the bilingual things'.[8]

The first group of Cuban teacher participants was given a year to complete the retraining program, which began at the UM in 1962.[9] They were also required to pass all of the state certification tests to teach in Florida, and all of the tests were given in English. Mackey and Beebe (1977) note that the Dade County school board made no exceptions when hiring non-credentialed teachers to work in either the school district or the bilingual program. However, Logan recognized that the bilingual school would require special personnel, and the summer teacher professional development program in 1962 and 1963 should include Cuban aides at Coral Way.

Sánchez describes the grueling nature of the retraining program itself: working at Coral Way until 6pm each night, staying after school to teach Spanish to local families, being fed by members of the local community, then heading to the UM for classes from 6:30pm until 11pm. To Sánchez, who was multilingual and already held a PhD in pedagogy, this was insulting: 'You know how many semesters we had to sit there?! From 6:30 at night to 11:00, and then rush home to be a mother, a wife, a teacher,

Image 3.1 Tita Piñeiro with a class of students around 1964. (*Source*: University of Florida Digital Collections.)

do the homework for the university, do the translating for the school, correct the papers of the kids'.

Gladys Margarita Diaz recalls her mother's hard work and commitment to the retraining program. The Cubans bonded to one another. She recalls, 'they interchanged a lot of information, they studied together, and I remember distinctly [proofreading] term papers that my mother would write. And I remember I was like in fifth or sixth grade, and I was the grammar person'.[10]

When her mother had term papers due, Gladys Margarita's mother and her friends hired her to proofread and type the papers. She would correct their papers, which she recalls as 'a very interesting flow, like the child correcting the parent, which is kind of funny'. The Cuban community of teachers was cohesive and connected. The teachers lived in close proximity to each other and worked as a group. Gladys Margarita recalls her mother's 'gang: they were all recertifying themselves in the United States – it was like a clump of people'.[11]

The tight-knit community of support saw successful outcomes. At the end of the year-long teacher education program, all 33 teachers passed the state certification test. Sánchez vividly recalls the moment when the teachers learned their test results:

> … very denigrating, that was all you were gonna get for those tests, a little piece of transparent paper, which said whether you made it or not. When [the director] came in, everybody froze, and I told everybody, 'He's gonna call out the names, and he's gonna flunk you. So don't you cry, don't you move – nothing. Don't anybody look at what you get. Let the person next to you look, and you just say, "You made it, you didn't make it"'. Out of thirty-three, thirty-three passed. That was the beginning of bilingual education at the University of Miami.[12]

Teacher Education

Summer 1963

The summer prior to 1963 was a landmark for the school and for on-site teacher education. Dade County schools instructed Logan to retain all of the English-speaking teachers at Coral Way unless they voluntarily chose to relocate to another school. This posed a problem, because he needed six native English-speaking teachers for the first year of the program. Only 4 of the original 12 English teachers requested transfers. However, once a mandatory summer training program was announced, through which all teachers would receive extensive preparation in working with non-native speakers, two additional teachers opted to leave. This opened up six teacher positions for Spanish-speaking teachers to balance the classrooms and follow the 50:50 model: six with native Spanish-speaking teachers and students, and six with native English-speaking students.

The summer workshop was six weeks long and was funded under the Cuban Refugee Program. The six selected Cuban aides, one of whom was Sánchez, reported to their prior year's school to assist ESL teachers in working with Cuban students. English-speaking teachers were required to report to a nearby school to receive preparation from Rosa Inclán, a consultant to Dade County schools and a former teacher at the Ruston Academy, an American school located in Havana that closed in 1961 (Conde, 1999). Inclán specialized in ESL teaching methods, and her work emphasized the bicultural component of the program, arguing that

> [t]he concepts of a pluralistic society, multi-ethnicity, and multicultural-ism were observed... as Dade County provided English instruction to the Cubans in addition to, and not to the detriment or suppression of, their own native Spanish proficiency. (Inclán, 1972: 192)

She continued that 'the problems of a low self-image and feelings of inadequacy due to cultural and language differences are averted through the Spanish-S [Spanish Language Arts for Spanish speakers] instructional program' (Inclán, 1972: 192). In other words, first language development had a positive effect on students' sense of self and identity.

During the afternoons, all 12 teachers, English and Spanish, reported to Coral Way where their primary focus was to analyze the existing curriculum, adapt the curriculum for English and Spanish medium instruction and discuss bilingual education procedures. The program had to be compatible with Florida state law, the Florida accreditation standards and Dade County school board policies. During this time, teachers began to identify the need for materials for Spanish-speaking students, and the particular ways that they would introduce literacy to those children.

The rationale for conducting (approximately) half of students' instruction through the medium of a second language, rather than entirely through one language such as English (a common misconception based on 'time-on-task', where more time in English would yield better outcomes) was based on prior research showing that children transfer skills from one language to another. This is what the Coral Way experiment ultimately aimed to assess. In addition, the experiment hypothesized that two different groups of students could acquire high levels of language and literacy in both languages in a model where two languages were used as mediums of instruction.

Materials were designed for students based on the audiolingual teaching method (Larsen-Freeman, 2011), a method of teaching language where students listen to a script or visual performance by a teacher, who models correct language use. At the time of the teacher education program, the audiolingual teaching method was considered a cutting-edge method for second language learning (see also Chapter 4). Repetitive behaviorism techniques were also promoted by Fries, a colleague of Rojas, who believed that intensive oral language drilling would support learning the basic patterns of language, particularly for young learners.

The aim of the workshop was to prepare teachers to teach their native language as a second language. Logan described the preparation as divided into two parts. In the morning, 12 teachers, 6 native English and 6 native Spanish, enrolled in 'Basic Linguistics' and 'Structures of the English Language'. In the afternoon, teachers worked in grade-level groups to develop the program and ensure its compliance with the scope and sequence of the Dade County curriculum. Logan described how teachers made 'hundreds of visual aids that were "finger-tip" filed for instant use' for the upcoming school year.[13]

Sánchez referred to the summer as development, because the Cuban aides were already teachers in Cuba. Teachers wrote learning objectives and learning goals, and developed whole classes of materials across subject matters and topics. Unlike the Spanish-speaking teachers, formerly Cuban aides, the English-speaking teachers did not attend the entire summer, because the curriculum in English already existed. They did need support in adapting their existing curriculum to the Spanish-speaking students. But, Piñeiro recalls, '[a]t the end of the day we were exhausted, because we had to plan and we had to make everything from scratch, because we didn't have the materials. That was the thing that was really a burden for us... the hard work. You have to love the program... you have to say "bilingual is great"'.[14]

Summer 1964

The following summer, a second six-week workshop was arranged for Coral Way teachers, both the trained Cuban aides who were then credentialed teachers and the English-speaking teachers in the program. The workshop was less focused on establishing teams of teachers to coordinate instruction, as during the summer of 1963, and more focused on the development of materials to support the bilingual curriculum. The teams were also provided with professional development to use technologies, mainly audio-video equipment, while continuing to support cross-cultural communication among teachers in and across the school teams.

Some of the equipment provided during the summer included over-head projectors, filmstrip projectors and dry-mount presses, considered novel and cutting-edge technologies in 1964. This contributed an air of innovation and novelty among the team. With knowledge of the equipment, the teams of teachers produced materials to use along with them. These included 24 acetates for the overhead projector and 203 dry-mounted pictures with cross-files to use as visual aids and to support the Fries language arts series. In addition, materials for the content areas were created: 199 'idea' cards for teaching mathematics from Grades 1 through 6; wet-mounted health and social studies charts using muslin (fabric); large felt animals for flannel board lessons and vowel sound charts for phonics lessons in the language arts; and charts for teaching parts of the body and clothing in health classes.

To establish the scope of the yearly curriculum, teachers devised individual lesson plans for their plan books, handbooks for teachers and long-range lesson plans. The 'culminating activity' for the summer was a Spanish fiesta, noted proudly on the report to the school district. Principal Logan noted that the English-speaking teachers would continue to take Spanish language lessons during the school year, and that the success of the summer workshop brought about 'a better understanding and acceptance of different cultures'.[15]

In sum, a key component in the establishment and implementation of the bilingual program model, and likely the most important resource, was the number of native Spanish-speaking teachers from Cuba who were already highly trained as teachers in Cuba and who were invested both personally and professionally in the bilingual education program. For some teachers, the opportunity to work as a Cuban aide or as a teacher was an opportunity to find employment in their career field in the south Florida context, where large numbers of immigrants were also searching for jobs. The bilingual Cuban aides played an essential role in the early years of the program by providing language support and filling other non-instructional duties, thereby allowing the teachers in the two-way program time to plan, revise and make collaborative decisions surrounding the curriculum and instruction for both the English- and the Spanish-speaking students.

In addition to the aides-turned-teachers, the English-speaking teach-ers were also heavily invested in the program. During summer, they were provided with six weeks of professional development in ESL methods, materials and curriculum. Both groups of teachers had strong leader-ship through Principal Logan and the special Ford Foundation team in Dade County, and supplemental on-site support through Cuban aides, enabling them to co-plan each day.

Notes

(1) Richardson, M.W. (1964, May 14) A study of certain aspects of the achievement of Coral Way Elementary pupils in the bilingual program. Unpublished project proposal. University of Florida Digital Collections. See https://ufdc.ufl.edu/AA00066042/00001.

(2) Sánchez-Pando, J. (2008, March 13) Interview by R. Ruiz [audio file]. Coral Way Elementary. University of Florida Digital Collections. See http://ufdc.ufl.edu/AA00065594/00001.

(3) Piñeiro, M. (2008, June 21) Interview by B. de Farber [audio file]. Coral Way Elementary. University of Florida Digital Collections. See https://ufdc.ufl.edu/AA00065593/00001.

(4) Gonzalez, O. (2008, March 26) Interview by R. Ruiz [audio file]. Coral Way Elementary. University of Florida Digital Collections. See https://ufdc.ufl.edu/AA00065599/00001.

(5) N.A. (c. 1963) Daily Schedules for Cuban Aides. See https://ufdc.ufl.edu/AA00066055/00001.

(6) See note 2.

(7) See note 2.

(8) See note 2.

(9) See note 2.

(10) See note 2 and San Miguel, G. (2013) Shapers of their destiny: A history of the education of Cuban children in the United States since 1959. *US-China Education Review* 3 (4), 276–281. Note that San Miguel's article states that the program began in 1963, not 1962 as Sánchez recalled and as Logan stated in his speech in Ann Arbor in 1964.

(11) Diaz, G.M. and Diaz, J.G. (2008, March 15) Interview by R. Ruiz [audio file]. Coral Way Elementary. University of Florida Digital Collections. See https://ufdc.ufl.edu/AA00065600/00001.

(12) See note 10.

(13) See note 2.

(14) Logan, J.L. (1964) Final report of the bilingual workshop (p. 2). University of Florida Digital Collections. See https://ufdc.ufl.edu/AA00066061/00001.

(15) See note 2.

(16) See note 13.

References

Bell, P.W. (1969) Bilingual education in an American elementary school. In H.H. Stern (ed.) *Languages and the Young School Child* (pp. 112–118). London: Oxford University Press.

Inclán, R.G. (1972) Can bilingual-bicultural education be the answer? *Educational Horizons* 50 (4), 192–196.

Larsen-Freeman, D. (2011) *Techniques and Principles in Language Teaching* (3rd edn). Oxford: Oxford University Press.

Mackey, W.F. and Beebe, V.N. (1977) *Bilingual Schools for a Bicultural Community: Miami's Adaptation to the Cuban Refugees*. Rowley, MA: Newbury House.

Pérez, L. (1986) Cubans in the United States. *The Annals of the American Academy of Political and Social Science* 487 (1), 126–137.

Way, H.W. and Haden, N.N. (1966) Estamos orgullos de estar juntos. *FEA Journal* April, p. 66.

4 The *Miami Linguistic Readers* and Curriculum Development

Bilingual education programs, similar to other strong educational programs, require a culturally relevant curriculum with learning objectives that align to and build upon students' backgrounds, rigorous academic content, well-prepared teachers, strong leaders (Palmer, 2018) and staff, and materials that support student learning (Coady *et al.*, 2007). In the prior chapters, I noted the role of teacher education for both the Cuban aides who became bilingual teachers at Coral Way and the English teachers of the school. In addition to trained teachers, a specialized curriculum and materials were needed to support students' learning through the medium of two languages. These two areas – teacher education and curriculum and materials development – were the main objectives of the Ford Foundation funding because, by 1963, additional movements toward language rights and education were being organized in other US states including Texas, New Mexico and New York (Escamilla, 2018; Fránquiz, 2018). The curriculum for the bilingual program had to include both language as a content area (that is, Spanish and English language arts and reading), as well as bilingual content in science, mathematics, social studies and health.

As Principal Logan noted in his 1964 report, the English-speaking teachers had comparatively less work to do in writing a new curriculum for the bilingual program, mainly because they already had a curriculum to follow and to teach. For the Spanish side of the Coral Way bilingual program, however, there was little curriculum to rely on. Some of the curriculum and materials needed to be created, and other curriculum and materials needed to be adapted. Some of the early curriculum for the Spanish side of the program was borrowed from Puerto Rico, and there is evidence to suggest that materials from Spain were also used. Mackey and Beebe (1977) recognize how publishing firms from Spain and

Latin American countries were the early suppliers of materials for the Spanish language program at Coral Way. By the late 1960s, these companies began to specialize in and import curricular materials in Spanish. The key resource for the bilingual experiment, however, remained 'the availability of a large number of trained teachers from Spanish-speaking backgrounds that were able to present the Spanish language program of the instructional program' (Mackey & Beebe, 1977: 78).

Audiolingual Method

During the 1960s, language teaching and learning began to rely heavily on the audiolingual method, which was considered cutting edge at the time. Richardson's 1964 dissertation proposal cited the work of scholar Wallace Lambert, who advocated second language learning for young students. Lambert argued that young learners had the capability to develop correct language patterns using structured and sequenced methods. Richardson notes that 'well established verbal habits can be modified under certain schedules of reinforcement, and man's abilities are not permanently fixed by hereditary background... the learning of languages should be shifted to early age levels' (Lambert, 1963, cited in Richardson, 1964: 12–13). Lambert's research and scholarship at that time suggested that language learning could be best achieved by young children when the process of language learning was sequenced and aligned to the various age levels of children (e.g. young children and adolescents). Moreover, the prevalent thinking in the 1960s was that young children up to the age of 10 could acquire a second language more quickly than adolescents (Penfield, 1963, as cited by Richardson, 1964: 12).

Some of the hallmark features of the audiolingual method included the need to establish strong oral (verbal) habits, sequence the language learning accordingly and drill language learning through oral repetition. The audiolingual method of teaching relied on structured oral sequencing and production (listening, repetition, drill), followed by the introduction of new words or grammatical structures that students, again, listened to, repeated and drilled. Richardson[1] cites then-contemporary scholars who promoted the audiolingual method (Carroll, 1962) and notes the characteristics of the method for foreign language learning:

(1) an adequate model of speech (oral language);
(2) methods that contrast the learner's language and the structure of the second language;
(3) drilling (oral) language patterns;

(4) student response in the target language that simulates 'real-life' situations and communication.

The audiolingual method was adapted for Coral Way's bilingual education program and the Spanish-speaking students' learning English as a second language (ESL), in contrast to English as a foreign language (EFL). In addition, students needed to build literacy in English. Thus, the audiolingual method was adapted into literacy-building activities and language arts development (reading and writing). An example of the use of the reader, *Nat the Rat* (Robinett, 1965), demonstrates how visual support, in this case from the book and characters, aligned with the audiolingual teaching methods, as in Figure 4.1. The teacher guide demonstrates how the teacher methods of oral language drill were aligned to the materials.

At the time, the audiolingual method was considered to be the ideal method for second language learning. Richardson noted that '[i]t may be that the audio-lingual method is appropriate for second language learning at very early levels for certain children' (Lambert, 1963, cited in Richardson, 1964: 13).

This is precisely what the *Miami Linguistic Readers* aimed to do. The readers were conceptualized in the first summer training program in 1963, before Coral Way opened its doors to the public. The readers were developed under the direction of Dr Pauline Rojas and in collaboration with Ralph Robinett during the summer of 1963, when teachers and aides worked together to create ESL literacy materials for the Spanish-speaking students. Thus, the readers targeted those students using a series of readers, teaching guides, big books and workbooks or 'seatbooks'. Rojas also had experience working with Charles Fries and the Fries reading series, which she had used in Puerto Rico. Paul Bell, Rojas's colleague in Dade County schools who also worked under the Ford Foundation grant, had also worked with the Fries series, and they were both strong advocates of the readers and believed in the methods.

The *Miami Linguistic Readers*

The early *Miami Linguistic Readers* were organized around seven levels of teaching reading to non-native English-speaking young children. The first, revised experimental 1965 series consisted of seven levels and included 10 books:

Level 1A: *Biff and Tiff*
Level 1B: *Kid Kit and the Catfish*

LANGUAGE

Structure emphasis
Inverted questions with <u>Is</u> <u>Is</u> (this, that) (Kid Kit)?
Affirmative and negative answers <u>No, it isn't</u>. <u>It's</u> (Nat the Rat).
What in questions with proper names <u>What is</u> (Nat)? <u>A</u> (rat).

Sample vocabulary	
Nat	rat
Kid Kit	cat
Miss Min	kitten
Biff	dog
Tiff	puppy
Sparky	
Speedy	

READING

Reading emphasis
Title <u>NAT the RAT</u>, <u>Nat the Rat</u>
Words <u>NAT</u>, <u>RAT</u>, <u>the</u>, <u>Nat</u>, <u>Rat</u>

BIG BOOK II, CHART 1

1. Show the pupils Chart 1 and tell them that the name of the rat is Nat. Guide them in asking <u>Is that (Kid Kit)</u>? and in answering <u>No, it isn't</u>, <u>It's Nat the Rat</u>, and <u>Yes, it is</u>, <u>It's Nat the Rat</u>. Then guide them to ask <u>What is (Nat)</u>? and to answer <u>A (rat)</u>. Follow techniques in <u>A</u>, <u>B</u> and <u>C</u> of the fold-out at the back of this manual.

    Teacher: (pointing to Nat on Chart 1)
               Is that Kid Kit?
    Group 1: Is that Kid Kit?
    Teacher: No, it isn't. It's Nat the Rat.
    Group 2: No, it isn't. It's Nat the Rat.
    Pupil 1: Is that Kid Kit?
    Pupil 2: No, it isn't. It's Nat the Rat.
    Help the pupils to pronounce <u>Nat</u> and <u>Rat</u> by having them smile as they say these words.

2. Have the pupils ask and answer the question <u>Is that (Nat the Rat)</u>? Have them substitute the names Kid Kit, Miss Min, Biff, Tiff, Sparky, Speedy, and a cat, a kitten, a dog, a puppy, as you show them pictures or puppets. Then have them practice asking <u>What is (Nat)</u>? using the names of the characters and answering <u>A (rat)</u> as they use the puppets or pictures.

3. Read the title on Chart 1 and guide the whole group, then small groups and individual pupils in reading it.

4. Write the title on the chalkboard in capital letters as it appears on the chart. Under it write the title capitalizing only <u>N</u> and <u>R</u>. Help the pupils observe the difference. Have them read.

5. Write the words <u>Nat</u> and <u>Rat</u> in a column on the chalkboard and have the pupils read each word as you point to it. Point to the words at random and have individual pupils read them and frame the part that is the same in both words and the part that is different. Then have them reread the title on Chart 1.

6. Have the pupils identify Nat the Rat on Seatwork page 3. Then have them color the picture, cut it out and paste it on a stick to make a puppet.

Figure 4.1 *Nat the Rat* (Teacher's manual)[2]

Level 2: *Nat the Rat*
Level 3: *Tug Duck and Buzz Bug*
Plateau (Levels 1–3): *The Sack Hut*

Level 4: *On the Rock in the Pond*
Level 5: *The Picnic Ship*
Level 6: *Hot Corn Muffins!*
Plateau (Levels 4–6): *The Camping Trip*

Level 7: *The Magic Bean*

Evident are the linguistic regularity and patterns that are introduced to children in the foregoing titles, where minimal pairs and linguistic regularity are introduced, subsequently followed by more complex linguistic patterns for children to decode.

In the preface to the readers, Robinett and the series developers describe the premises upon which the readers were developed: the series should be interesting to the child, reflect natural language forms of children's speech, have listening and speaking control of the material she/he is expected to read and that there should be strict control (in the readers and by the teachers) of the vocabulary and grammatical structures. In addition, the focus of the materials should be on the 'skills involved... rather than on the uses to which reading is put' (*Nat the Rat*; Robinett, 1965: 3) and students should experience progressive success as they master the materials.

Sánchez believed that the *Miami Linguistic Readers* series was groundbreaking. 'What came out of that series', she states, 'was the best series that I have seen for a non-North American-English-speaking person to learn how to read'. Sánchez felt that the books were successful because the languages, English and Spanish, required different teaching methods due to their different phonological or sound systems. 'These books were written to attack the problems of hearing, that the Spanish child has, that the North American child does not. Because in the development of his language at home, [the North American child] picks up the short "I" and the long "I" immediately, because "my shoes don't fit on my feet"'.[3]

Sánchez continues that the early series of readers dealt with only one vowel sound in the whole reader. 'Nat the rat saw a fat cat....."Biff and Tiff." Biff is a dog, like.... Let me see what he would be. He's a mutt, who is the father of Tiff. And Tiff is a very mischievous little dog that does all sorts of bad things that you can do in English with a short ĭ... and it's just a tiny reader'.[4]

The contrast between Spanish- and English-speaking students who learn to read differs because the English speakers hear English for years before learning to read the language. Hence, they have a well-established oral language system of words that they rely on and on which they learn to connect symbols (letters and then words).

The entire series was developed by Dade County schools and the Coral Way teachers, in collaboration with reading consultants and with funding from the Ford Foundation.[5] The books were written, printed and eventually recorded with songs associated with the materials. Sánchez recalled, 'We couldn't afford anything but black-and-white. And they were very good black-and-white books. Added one dab of color to the book. I remember *Nat the Rat* had red. And *Tuck Duck* had brown... That magnificent project, that was done by people who knew the differences in the language, because they could speak both of them'.[6]

There is no doubt that the readers, though eventually gaining some notoriety in the academic literature (Criscuolo, 1970), were intended for students in the then-only two-way bilingual education program. The teacher's manual notes that the structured program of language learning, that is, the use of readers in classrooms, would be accompanied by an 'unstructured English language activities' during the school day by 'bilingual and culturally disadvantaged pupils' who were in the process of learning English (Criscuolo, 1970: 4). In other words, the *Miami Linguistic Readers* aimed to support bilingual students but the program recognized that other language use, that is, unstructured language time, was necessary to build the oral bilingual abilities of students.

Criscuolo (1970) examined the readers in 1970, noting the rise in the number of readers in the United States used to teach reading at that time. He suggested that the increase in the number of reading series, and the subsequent academic articles (44) on the use of readers to teach reading in school, was a direct result of Chall's (1983) work.

Chall (1983) had studied the effect of learning to read by decoding language as opposed to following a whole language approach that used basal readers where students learned high frequency words. Chall found that decoding language into its smaller linguistic parts and according to a specific sequence was beneficial to children learning to read. More specifically, she noted that children benefit from learning linguistically regular patterns. One example of teaching linguistically regular patterns is minimal pairs in reading instruction. Minimal pairs are words that differ in only one consonant or vowel, such as nat and rat, or biff and tiff, both of which differ only in the initial consonant position, n/r and b/t. Those two minimal pairs were the names of the first books developed in the *Miami Linguistic Readers* series.

Cultural References

New, additional reading materials for ESL students continued to be developed and piloted across Texas, New Mexico, Arizona and

Colorado, as well as in Puerto Rico.[7] Not all of the groups were Spanish speakers. The Arizona pilot was purported to have taken place with native Americans as well.[8] As an ESL curriculum, the materials were intended to illustrate traditional 'American' culture, which was directly related to the Coral Way objective numbers (3), (5) and (7) in Chapter 1:

3. He will be able to operate in either culture easily and comfortably.
5. In general terms, he will be more acceptive of strange people and cultures and will thus increase the range of his job opportunities.
7. He will broaden his understanding of people and the world and be able to live a richer fuller and more satisfying personal life.[9]

Cultural references in the readers included *The Magic Bean*, a Level 7 reader that was adapted from the English fairy tale, *Jack and the Beanstalk* and *The White Horse*, a Level 13 reader adapted from a Navajo tale, with the permission of Dr LeRoy Condie.

Following Coral Way's structured curriculum and the separation of languages, English and Spanish, for instructional purposes, only one of the readers appears to have used both English and Spanish in the same book. The plateau reader for Levels 10–12 is titled *B is for Bicycle*. The book describes Carlos Perez, a 12-year-old, Spanish-speaking boy from a migrant farmworking family. Carlos is invited by his father to travel for the first time to pick crops. Upon arriving in the town, Carlos spots a new bicycle, which he is immediately enamored with and seeks to buy with the money he earns from picking crops. Despite a frost that destroys the tomatoes, Carlos manages to find the additional money needed to purchase the bicycle.

Carlos is decidedly from a Mexican background in this story. The images in the story reveal Mexican hats, the women's dresses, pueblo architecture and the known mariachi song, *Cielito Lindo*. Carlos speaks Spanish to only his mother, 'Si, mamá. Ya voy' and 'hasta luego, mama', and she speaks to Carlos only in Spanish (Figure 4.2).

Gladys Margarita Diaz recalls the emphasis on learning about non-Cuban cultural groups, and dressing up using authentic costumes from Latin American countries. She recalls that 'Mrs. Benitez was very adamant about making sure that not only did we understand Cuban culture, but we got social studies in every single Latin American culture, and to really appreciate the history of Ecuador, the history of Colombia, the history of Venezuela – just so that it's a pan-Hispanic viewpoint, as opposed to just this sort of "I am Cuban and that's all I am"'.[10]

Figure 4.2 B is for Bicycle

Sánchez, who taught the Spanish renaissance, used materials from Spain when teaching artist Velasquez and El Greco. In the early days of the program, teachers created their own materials, borrowed materials from Spain or translated materials from the English curriculum into Spanish.

The cultural references in the readers seemed limited to native American people, Mexican and English, and, ironically, there are no early cultural references to Cuban culture or Cuban language uses in the stories of the initial series, Books 1–7. The limited bilingual language use in the books, as well as the distinct cultural groups such as Mexicans, who are stereotyped as poor and working class, and mothers who are non-English speaking, are among some of the materials that comprised the reading curriculum for Spanish-speaking students.

Students in the first classes of Coral Way similarly recalled the cultural component of their academic curriculum. Bess de Farber recalled songs that students were required to memorize to learn language and culture: 'We were learning all of the songs... for all of the [United States] military: the navy, the army, the marines. We were learning all of the songs for those military service groups in English. And "The Battle Hymn of the Republic" and "America the Beautiful"'.

de Farber recalled that the students seemed to have learned equal amounts of songs in Spanish, but they were primarily singers of songs from Cuba with Cuban cultural references. She continued that the Cuban aide would teach the students the Spanish songs, and 'most of them, I believe were of Cuban origin, because my mother [who was from Argentina] didn't know them'. She vividly recalled *El Ratoncito Miguel*, by Félix Benjamín Miguel (Cuba, 1892–1976) and *El Manicero*, The Peanut Vendor, by Moises Simons (Cuba, 1889–1945). Gladys Margarita recalled Cuban hymns, particularly the Cuban independence song of 1902, *El Veinte de Mayo*. The use of songs reinforced a sense of Cuban identity among students, because they represented the majority of Spanish speakers and the cultural background of the Cuban aides.

Curriculum for English-Speaking Students

One early concern of parents of English-speaking children was the issue of ensuring that their children received adequate instruction through the medium of English so that they did not fall behind in academic subjects comparable to their peers in English-only schools. In the spring of 1963, Mr Logan held a series of meetings with parents to assuage their concerns.[11] Bell (1969: 115) wrote that in addition to the ESL component, described earlier, 'Science was given special attention because the availability of parallel texts in English and Spanish made it possible to sharpen the science concepts through their study'. In other words, Spanish and English share similar Latin word roots, and these are especially evident in the area of science. Hence, the curriculum could quite easily support both languages through science and the concepts could be readily reinforced.

Other areas that required attention by the teachers in their pre-planning during 1963 as well as during the academic school year, within the one-hour daily planning sessions, were music, art and PE. Bell (1969: 115) reasoned that these were given attention because in those areas, 'intracultural relations would initially be the greatest'. State-adopted textbooks were selected for the English curriculum, and Spanish translations of the science text were adopted, along with Spanish curriculums in health and mathematics.

For Spanish language arts for the English-speaking students, Dade County ordered four series of texts: a basal reader series in Spanish, a

Spanish translation of the county's science text, a Spanish health text series and a Spanish mathematics series. Bell (1969: 116) notes that all of these materials were published in the United States and reflected modern American pedagogy in their approach and content. Logan's report was more specific with respect to the publishers of the Spanish language materials for English speakers. His report noted:

Laidlaw (Health and Readers)
D.C. Heath (Miami Linguistic Readers, Science, Fries American-English Series
Silver-Burdett (Math)
Follett (Library Books)[12]

Ultimately, the Spanish language curriculum for English-speaking students at Coral Way was conceptualized and created by the Cuban, Spanish teachers and supported through texts and materials by Dade County schools. The *Miami Linguistic Readers* were intended for ESL students following the audiolingual method of second language learning. The readers were books and materials meant to support reading in English. Culturally, the readers aimed to introduce students to 'American culture', but the Spanish teachers introduced curriculum that reflected pan-Hispanic culture.

Notes

(1) Richardson, M.W. (1964, May 14) A study of certain aspects of the achievement of Coral Way Elementary pupils in the bilingual program. Unpublished project proposal. University of Florida Digital Collections. See https://ufdc.ufl.edu/AA00066042/00001.

(2) The *Miami Linguistic Readers* were published by DC Heath between 1964 and the 1970s. DC Heath corporation was sold to Houghton Mifflin, which was then purchased under the umbrella of the Nelson Group publishing companies. The Nelson Group claims that the materials are owned by Oxford University Press, but Oxford University Press states that they do not own, nor do they have knowledge of, the materials.

(3) Sánchez-Pando, J. (2008, March 13) Interview by R. Ruiz [audio file]. Coral Way Elementary. University of Florida Digital Collections. See http://ufdc.ufl.edu/AA00065594/00001.

(4) See note 3.

(5) Mackey and Beebe note that the Cuban Refugee Program was funded by the Ford Foundation. They note that the refugee program actually paid for the development of the *Miami Linguistic Readers*.

(6) See note 2.

(7) Rojas, P. (1966, August 25) Final report: Ford Foundation projects in bilingual education, Dade County Public Schools (p. 43). Ford Foundation Archives. *The School Board of Dade County, Florida* (06300064). 17 December 1962 to 16 December 1965.

(8)   See note 7, p. 46.
(9)   See note 7 and Logan, J.L. (c. 1964) Coral Way: A Bilingual School Speech. University of Florida Digital Collections. See https://ufdc.ufl.edu/AA00066053/00001.
(10) Diaz, G.M. and Diaz, J.G. (2008, March 15) Interview by R. Ruiz [audio file]. Coral Way Elementary. University of Florida Digital Collections. See https://ufdc.ufl.edu/AA00065600/00001.
(11) Logan, J.L. (1963, April 14) Letter to all parents of first- and second-grade pupils. University of Florida Digital Collections. See https://ufdc.ufl.edu/AA00066047/00001.
(12) Logan, J.L. (c. 1964) Coral Way: A Bilingual School Speech. University of Florida Digital Collections. See https://ufdc.ufl.edu/AA00066053/00001 and Rojas, P. and Robinett, R. (1963, October 29) A report: Progress report on Ford Foundation Projects. University of Florida Digital Collections. See https://ufdc.ufl.edu/AA00066059/00001.

References

Bell, P.W. (1969) Bilingual education in an American elementary school. In H.H. Stern (ed.) *Languages and the Young School Child* (pp. 112–118). London: Oxford University Press.

Carroll, J.B. (1962) Research on teaching foreign languages. In N.L. Gage (ed.) *Handbook on Research on Teaching* (pp. 1060–1061). Chicago, IL: Rand McNally.

Chall, J.S. (1983) *Stages of Reading Development*. New York: McGraw Hill.

Coady, M., Hamann, E.T., Harrington, M., Pacheco, M., Pho, S. and Yedlin, J. (2007) Successful schooling for ELLs: Principles for building responsive learning environments. In L.S. Verplaetse and N. Migliacci (eds) *Inclusive Pedagogy for English Language Learners: A Handbook of Research-Informed Practices* (pp. 245–255). New York: Lawrence Erlbaum Associates.

Criscuolo, N.P. (1970) A look at linguistic readers. *Reading Horizons* 10 (3), 115–119.

Escamilla, K. (2018) Growing up with the Bilingual Education Act: One educator's journey. *Bilingual Research Journal* 41 (4), 369–387.

Fránquiz, M. (2018) The Bilingual Research Journal: Dreams, possibilities, and necessity. *Bilingual Research Journal* 41 (4), 344–368.

Lambert, W.E. (1963) Psychological approaches to the study of language learning and bilingualism. *Modern Language Journal* 47, 114–121.

Mackey, W.F. and Beebe, V.N. (1977) *Bilingual Schools for a Bicultural Community: Miami's Adaptation to the Cuban Refugees*. Rowley, MA: Newbury House.

Palmer, D.K. (2018) *Teacher Leadership for Social Change in Bilingual and Bicultural Education*. Bristol: Multilingual Matters.

Penfield, W. (1963) *Handbook on Research on Teaching*. New York: Rand McNally Co.

Richardson, M. (1968) An evaluation of certain aspects of the academic achievement of elementary pupils in a bilingual program. Unpublished doctoral dissertation, University of Miami.

Robinett, R.N. (1965) *Nat the Rat*. Miami Linguistic Readers. Boston: DC Heath.

5 Did it Work? Findings from the Coral Way Experiment

To return to the main focus of this book, the first bilingual education program at Coral Way Elementary was as much a social experiment as it was an educational experiment in student learning. The initial seven goals of the program illuminated a wide array of objectives that could only be measured using quantitative and qualitative assessments, as well as longitudinal assessments of student and community satisfaction and social outcomes over a long period of time. For instance, Dade County school district's commitment to the Ford Foundation was to examine language proficiency levels in English and Spanish for both groups of students and to gauge student learning outcomes in mathematics and reading on the Stanford Achievement Test (SAT). Principal Logan, however, did not rely exclusively on student achievement data to determine the Coral Way's success. Logan described the initial and subsequent demand for the program as a marker of the program's positive outcomes.

As noted in Chapter 1, the educators of Dade County schools and Coral Way's leaders and visionaries outlined seven goals for the bilingual program: equivalent learning for bilingual students as compared to monolingual students from similar backgrounds; students language ability in two languages; student biculturalism; enhanced objectivity in thinking; increased vocational or job potential; and cross-cultural understanding, which they theorized, would lead to a more satisfying personal life. The seven original goals of the experiment were

1. The participating pupil will have achieved as much in the way of skills, abilities and understandings as he would have had he attended a monolingual school.
2. He will be approximately as proficient in his second language (within his educational level) as he is in his first language. If he is a skilled reader in his first language, he will be a skilled reader in his second

language. If he has mastered the fundamental processes and concepts in arithmetic in one language, he will handle them equally in the second language. If he can express himself clearly and adequately in his first language, he will be able to do likewise in the other language. If he understands and uses concepts in science and social studies, he will handle these concepts equally in both languages.

3. He will be able to operate in either culture easily and comfortably.

4. He will have acquired consciously or unconsciously an understanding of the symbolic nature of language and as a result will be able to achieve greater objectivity in his thinking processes.

5. In general terms, he will be more acceptive of strange people and cultures and will thus increase the range of his job opportunities.

6. He will have skills, abilities and understandings which will greatly extend his vocational potential and thus increase his usefulness to himself end the world in which he lives.

7. He will broaden his understanding of people and the world and be able to live a richer fuller and more satisfying personal life.[1]

Goals 1 and 2

Although Coral Way was an innovative experiment and the program's consultants were leading scholars, educators and policymakers at the time, there are surprisingly few sources of data on student learning outcomes to demonstrate the achievement of students who participated in the program. The first two goals included quantitative measures related to students' bilingualism and biliteracy development. Among the few and most detailed reports was a research study conducted by Mabel Wilson Richardson. Richardson, originally from Georgia, had been trained as a schoolteacher and taught elementary education in Dade County schools beginning in 1950. She received a master of education degree from the University of Miami in 1961 and worked at Coral Way as a reading resource teacher in 1961–1962.[2] In 1962, Richardson was Bess de Farber's first-grade teacher, a year before the bilingual program began, but she was present during its conceptualization.

Richardson subsequently enrolled at the University of Miami in a doctorate in education program. She had ongoing access to students in the Coral Way program and worked with school administrators to design, identify and collect data. In addition, educational policymakers and foreign language specialists such as Bruce Gaardner urgently communicated with Richardson to gain access to her study's findings. Gaardner wrote about the 'great need'[3] for her findings to be released as soon as possible, particularly around six areas. First, Gaardner asked for information to guide educational policy; second, he wanted to learn about the bilingual development of Spanish speakers, especially differentiating by amount of time the students had been enrolled in the program; third, he sought data on English speakers' proficiency in Spanish; fourth, he asked about the adverse effects of bilingual education; fifth, Gaardner wanted to know if the tests of language and achievement (the Cooperative Inter-American Tests and the SAT) were adequate. Finally, he aimed to learn about differences across the two language groups of students.

Richardson's dissertation aimed to investigate the achievement of students participating in the Coral Way experiment. In her original dissertation proposal written in 1964, Richardson sought to collect data from Grades 1 to 3 students using the SAT and parallel English and Spanish language proficiency levels using the Cooperative Inter-American Test. She also aimed at the time to audio record individual participating students, focusing on academic vocabulary as a way to determine students' language proficiency in the content areas. The instrument, an interview protocol, was to be designed in collaboration with teachers from the school.

Richardson's original design did not manifest as she proposed. In the 1968 dissertation report, however, Richardson presents data on student learning from a three-year period. She notes the collection of data using the SAT and the Cooperative Inter-American Test. The Cooperative Inter-American Test consists of two parts: a general ability test and a reading test. Richardson used only the reading test in her dissertation.[4] No interviews with students, faculty, staff or parents were conducted or referenced in her dissertation study findings.

In the final design of her study, which by 1966 (which is the date of Gaardner's letter) had attracted some initial attention, Richardson had designed her dissertation study by grouping students into three categories: Group A, Group B and Group C. Group A consisted of both English-speaking and Spanish-speaking students who attended Coral Way (the intervention group, which she refers to as the 'experiment' group) and students who did not attend Coral Way (the match sample or 'control' group) in the first, second and third grades. Group B consisted of both English-speaking and Spanish-speaking students who attended Coral Way (the intervention) and students who did not attend Coral Way (the match) in second, third and fourth grades. Group C consisted of both English-speaking and Spanish-speaking students who attended Coral Way (the intervention) and students who did not attend Coral Way (the match) in third, fourth and fifth grades. These represented

Years 1, 2 and 3 of the program or 1963–1964, 1964–1965 and 1965–1966, respectively, of the study.

Each group of students was therefore subcategorized according to his or her native language. However, as indicated in Chapter 2 of this book, reports from Principal Logan indicated that groups of students were much more fluid and 'shifting' than the staff had originally anticipated, and subsequent changes to the model occurred. This was in large part due to the increasing number of Spanish-speaking students who relocated into the Coral Way neighborhood, particularly those who had some education in the United States and whose literacy levels in English were higher than teachers' originally thought. There was also the teacher and staff's difficulty in determining students' placement or morning vernacular classes, because they did not rely on screeners or tests.

Table 5.1 shows Richardson's groupings of students for the study. The need to assign students to different groupings was partly attributed to the different versions of the SAT or Cooperative Inter-American Test that they needed to take each year. In other words, depending on the grade level, different versions of tests needed to be administered (students cannot take the same test each year). In addition, each group attended Coral Way at a different starting point in the program (first, second or third grade) and was tested after a period of three years. Thus, the three different groups had different start and end dates in the experiment, based on grade levels (first through third, second through fourth or third through fifth grade). Table 5.1 demonstrates the total number of students who participated in Richardson's study.

The five subtests of the SAT were similar across the three different groups of students (A, B and C), despite the various versions of the test administered. For example, according to Richardson's data, all students were tested on 'paragraph meaning', which was a test of reading comprehension, 'word meaning' and 'spelling'. In mathematics, all students were tested on 'arithmetic reasoning' and 'computation'.

Table 5.1 Student groupings and number of students for analytic purposes (1963–1966)

	Group A: Grades 1–3		Group B: Grades 2–4		Group C: Grades 3–5	
	English	Spanish	English	Spanish	English	Spanish
Intervention group	36	31	33	38	40	38
Match sample group	36	33	23	35	33	38
Total students	72	64	56	73	73	76

The Dade County schools' regular testing program included the SAT; the Otis Alpha test, which was administered to students in the third grade; and the California Mental Maturity test, which was administered to students in the fifth grade. Students were administered the district-wide tests in October of each year, so data from those fall assessments were included in Richardson's findings. Because those tests were administered across the district, Richardson had access to the data from the match sample group of students.

Richardson's Findings on Academic Achievement

In addition to student grades on report cards, the academic achievement of the Coral Way students was measured using the SAT across all groups (A, B and C), as well as with the match sample. The Coral Way Spanish language teachers were intense and unwavering in their delivery of Spanish. As seen on Carol Shore's report card (see Chapter 2), they were militant in ensuring that students were learning to read and write in the second language and neither afraid to administer low grades in Spanish, nor hesitant in offering home suggestions to support language learning. This was a main objective of the Coral Way experiment and teachers ensured that the objective would be met.

But student achievement across the different groups of students needed to be calculated in order to ascertain the overall effectiveness of the program, whether students were able to learn academic content in two languages, and if they performed *as well as* their peers in mono-lingual English-only programs. Twelve tables of data were prepared by Richardson in her dissertation study to demonstrate the achievement across the various groups of students. She used mean or average test scores for each group of students (A, B and C) and across each of the five subtests (paragraph meaning, word meaning, spelling, arithmetic reasoning and arithmetic computation). She computed the standard deviation across the various subtests and groups, and she also conducted *t*-tests to determine statistical differences across the groups.

Findings from Richardson's (1968: 61) study revealed that English-speaking students in the intervention group (that is, those students who attended Coral Way) in 1967 were 'somewhat superior' in achievement compared to the match sample group (presumably those attending Auburndale Elementary) at the end of Year 1. This includes students from all groups (A, B and C) overall. However, the English-speaking students' higher scores diminished over the three-year period, leaving both groups (the Coral Way intervention and the Auburndale match groups) about equivalent in learning outcomes.

Group C students, that is, those students who were tested in Grades 3–5 and attended Auburndale, the match sample school, had significantly higher achievement on the subtests in all three years, but the difference in achievement lessened or diminished over time across the groups. In other words, English-speaking students who were instructed entirely through English (the match sample at Auburndale) performed better in English than English-speaking students in the intervention group at Coral Way. However, across the three-year study period, students in the Coral Way bilingual program, whether English speaking or Spanish speaking, performed *at least as well* as the English- and Spanish-speaking students in the monolingual, match sample school.

This finding, albeit not hair-raising today, was a welcome and confirmatory outcome of the school district's first hypothesis, which was that students in the bilingual program would do *at least as well* as students not in the bilingual program. In other words, learning through two different languages of instruction would not hinder students' academic achievement (namely, reading and mathematics performance).

Language Proficiency

To determine the students' language abilities in English and Spanish, Richardson used the Cooperative Inter-American Test, which was administered in May of each year of the study (1964, 1965 and 1966). Richardson utilized the forms of the test that focused on reading (analogies and comprehension).

The Cooperative Inter-American test assesses five grade levels of students. Level 1 corresponds loosely to kindergarten and Grade 1 students; Level 2 corresponds to Grades 2 and 3 students; and Level 3 corresponds to Grades 4 through 6. Older students can take Levels 4 and 5 of the test. There are six separate parts to the test. Four parts relate to oral and written language (sentence completion, world relations, analogies and classification). These four parts determine a verbal and non-verbal score. Two parts relate to numbers (computation and number series), and when combined yield a numerical score. Richardson did not state if she used all or which of these subtests and scores she used to determine language proficiency in English and Spanish.

The Cooperative Inter-American Reading Test was created, piloted and validated with Spanish-speaking students from Puerto Rico[5] and not students from Cuban backgrounds. This is important, particularly in reading vocabulary, because Cuban Spanish and Puerto Rican Spanish are mutually intelligible languages, that is, speakers of one language can generally understand speakers of the other, but they can use different vocabulary words (Zentella, 1990).

We do not know the extent to which teachers accounted for the varieties of Spanish being used, but students at Coral Way recall extensive and tedious vocabulary drilling. Feinberg later used the readers for a very short period of time in her middle school English to speakers of other languages (ESOL) classroom.[6] She describes the readers as boring and no fun at all, for both herself as the teacher and for her students.

Richardson noted in her dissertation study that 'concepts... taught in the native language... were reinforced in the second language in the afternoon'. Thus, there was an alignment of the curriculum across both languages and dedicated co-planning time for teachers to ensure that content learning was covered in one or both languages. In the afternoons, teachers began their lesson by teaching 'additional vocabulary necessary for the understanding the concepts [sic]',[7] but they assumed that most of the vocabulary had been taught.

Richardson compared the language proficiency levels of both Spanish- and English-speaking students on tests of Spanish and English that were considered comparable or parallel tests (Table 5.2). As expected, all groups of students (A, B, and C) increased their language abilities in both languages across all years. In other words, all of the students at Coral Way, whether in the English- or Spanish-speaking group, performed better in Year 2 than Year 1, and they performed better in Year 3 than Year 2. Growth across both languages was therefore evident and students were not stunted in their language ability in either language.

However, performance in the second languages across the two student groups differed. For Spanish-speaking students, their performance in English was consistently higher in the second language (English) than the performance of the English-speaking students' in Spanish. In other words, the Spanish speakers attained a higher language ability level in their second language, English, than the English-speaking students in their second language, Spanish. Richardson reasoned that this may have occurred because the Spanish speakers had greater incentive to learn English, for both communicative purposes in the community and for academic purposes in school, and they had more opportunities to practice the second language compared to the English speakers. These remain important differences between learning English as a second language, as in Coral Way, and learning English as a foreign language as taught in countries where English is not the main language of communication.

Importantly, according to Richardson, was that the English-speaking students were learning a second language and acquiring literacy in that

Table 5.2 Coral Way student language achievement on the Cooperative Inter-American Tests

	Years in Program	Spanish	English
Spanish-speaking groups			
A (Grades 1–3)	1	36.38	21.52
	2	54.33	44.86
	3	75.84	64.45
B (Grades 2–4)	1	53.76	64.45
	2	79.79	47.63
	3	94.30	72.37
C (Grades 3–5)	1	71.41	50.16
	2	84.92	79.68
	3	96.71	91.39
English-speaking groups			
A (Grades 1–3)	1	19.51	42.69
	2	40.00	58.78
	3	47.94	91.97
B (Grades 2–4)	1	25.71	57.09
	2	43.26	90.74
	3	53.60	100.11
C (Grades 3–5)	1	37.58	94.85
	2	59.32	104.76
	3	69.65	110.85

Source: Adapted from Richardson (1968).
Note: Mean scores by group.

language, and the Spanish-speaking students were learning to read and write in their native language, two benefits that were a direct result of the bilingual program. Richardson (1968: 63) describes the benefits as a 'valuable bonus' for the community. A second bonus was that the English-speaking students had an opportunity to learn a foreign language at a younger age than would normally have been offered.

What Richardson's Achievement Data Did *Not* Show

Richardson's study did not provide data for the Spanish-speaking students who attended the traditional, all-English school as the match sample group. We know that the Spanish speakers at Coral Way performed relatively well in Spanish and in English, compared to the native

English speakers in the same school, but we do not know how the match sample group of Spanish or English speakers performed in a second language (English or Spanish, respectively), because the Cooperative Inter-American Test was not administered to those students.

From Table 5.2 it seems that both groups of Coral Way students continued to make learning gains in both languages, but to varying and relative degrees. Yet, we do not know the degree of significance of differences across the groups. Richardson conducted the analyses of students' language proficiency using a *summary* of the mean scores for each group and for each year (as opposed to individual scores), but she did not conduct inferential statistics before drawing conclusions that there was a 'significant difference' in learning across groups over time. Because there are limited data on student means and number of participants, a post-study inferential test of significance could not be conducted.

In his early announcement to the media about the outcomes from students at Coral Way, Superintendent Joe Hall announced that some of the student performance was 'outstanding' while other performance was not as robust.[8] At that time, Hall noted the district's intention to study the language program in the upcoming 1964–1965 school year. A later news article, dated 16 August 1964, described the outcomes from students as 'better than average' for the school system,[9] and this sentiment contributed to a positive Coral Way environment. This echoed reports from Principal Logan, who reported back to the Ford Foundation and the Dade County administrators that the success of the program was evident from skeptical parents, who initially opted out of the program, but later chose to enroll their child. Logan wrote, 'perhaps a better indication of the success... [is] that after one year of offering the bilingual programme, the parents of the pupils who were in traditional classes requested that their children be moved into the bilingual programme' (Bell, 1969: 117).

Despite that resounding positive public pronouncement, scholars of education today would likely analyze data on student achievement differently than Richardson did in 1968. For example, in modern statistics a good practice is to apply data visualization to data sets when presenting data. A line chart would provide a direct visual path both to view the growth trajectory of the test scores over time and to illuminate the differences between the intervention and the match sample groups. A data chart for each of the five subtests (three language arts and two mathematics) is helpful.

Second, statistical analysis of achievement data should use a test of analysis of variance (ANOVA) or an analysis of covariance (ANCOVA) to determine differences among the groups. It is possible that Richardson added test scores for each individual student and created a total test score. She then may have conducted an ANCOVA to identify differences between the groups. This procedure may account for the overall F score provided in her dissertation findings.

In addition, it appears that she conducted a t-test of statistical significance before conducting an F test. An F test would identify statistical differences among at least three groups, which Richardson had in the data (Groups A, B and C). This would normally be followed by a t-test to determine which pair(s) have statistically significant outcomes.

Finally, a robust analysis would include accounting for the effect of the intervention over time. For instance, after identifying student differences in achievement, a series of ANOVA or ANCOVA statistical procedures should be conducted to identify if there are significant effects of treatment over time. It would also be helpful to know if there were significant differences in achievement in different years or whether student achievement growth was a function of time.

Re-Presenting Richardson's Data (1962–1966)

Using Dr Richardson's data from her 1968 dissertation, data visualizing techniques were applied to illuminate her findings more clearly. Figures 5.1–5.5 are reanalyzed data from the SAT administered to the three groups of students (that is, Groups A, B and C), and further separated by English speaking and Spanish speaking. The data from the SAT were collected by Richardson between 1962 and 1963 (as pre-test data with Groups B and C) and 1965 to 1966. Each figure represents the five variables that Richardson analyzed in her dissertation using data obtained from the SAT. Because Richardson included standard deviations, we are able to see the range of scores and the standard deviations across each group. The vertical bars within the graphs represent the range of error from one standard deviation above the mean to one standard deviation below the mean. Scholars will note large standard deviations in the data, but we have no explanation in the dissertation of why these are large.

Figure 5.1 demonstrates student learning in 'paragraph meaning'. The left axis represents the average scores for each group, ranging from 10 to 50. The 'experiment' group is the group of students receiving the intervention (that is, those who attended Coral Way) and the 'control' group is the group of students who did not attend Coral Way. Importantly, across each of the five tables of individual achievement variables, Group A does not have a pretest score like Groups B and C. This is because Group A students began the program in first grade and no

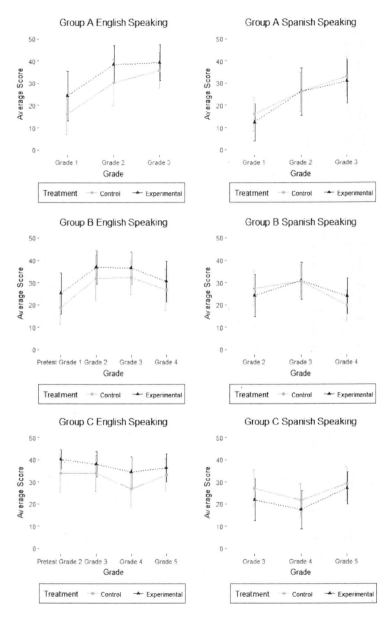

Figure 5.1 Student achievement on paragraph meaning

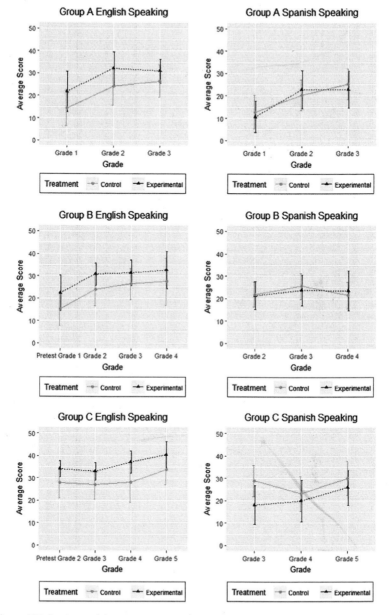

Figure 5.2 Student achievement on word meaning

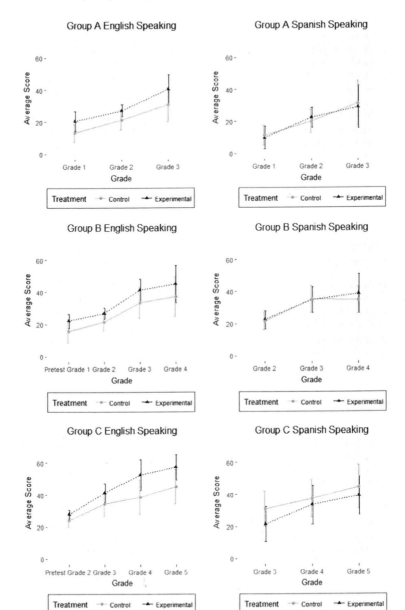

Figure 5.3 Student achievement on spelling

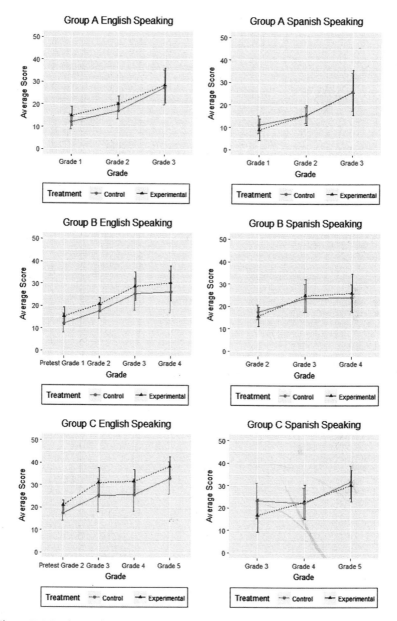

Figure 5.4 Student achievement on arithemetic reasoning

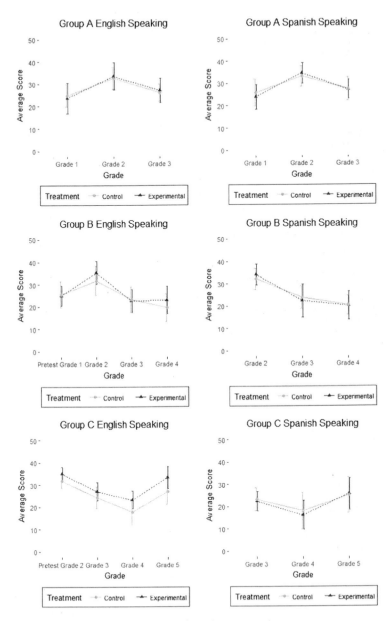

Figure 5.5 Student achievement on arithmetic computation

SAT data were available from the prior year; the test is only administered beginning in Grade 1.

Figure 5.1 demonstrates insightful trend lines. Readers can clearly see that the English-speaking group of students appeared to outperform the Spanish-speaking students overall in paragraph meaning, which is a component of reading comprehension. This is not surprising because the English-speaking students in all cases (including Grade 1 students) likely had all of their prior education through the medium of English. In addition, English-speaking students are surrounded by English in their homes, neighborhoods, communities and society, and on television and other media every day. However, in the area of paragraph meaning (Figure 5.1), both groups of students demonstrate slumped reading comprehension scores in fourth grade. Nationally, this phenomenon occurs in fourth-grade reading when students' transition from 'learning to read' to 'reading to learn' (Chall, 1983; Kitson, 2011; Møller *et al.*, 2014). Students in Coral Way and in the match sample groups were no different from national trends in reading.

It is important to also see the score differences between the Coral Way and non-Coral Way groups. English-speaking Coral Way students, for instance, outperform the match sample students for all three groups (A, B and C). These data are denoted with the dashed line in Figures 5.1–5.5. The differences between the Spanish-speaking match sample and the intervention students are smaller than those of the English-speaking students, and their scores seem roughly equivalent (and likely non-statistically significant).

Word meaning average scores follow similar observations and trends previously noted. Figure 5.2 demonstrates that among the English-speaking groups of students (A, B and C), the Coral Way group, denoted by a dashed line, performs better (scores higher) than the non-Coral Way group. The differences for the Spanish-speaking groups of students are not as wide. Similarly, spelling scores among the three groups (A, B and C) and across the Coral Way and non-Coral Way students are lower overall for the Spanish speakers than they are for the English speakers. In other words, the English speakers continue to perform slightly better than the Spanish speakers, and the English-speaking Coral Way students perform the highest across all of the groups, on average.

Figures 5.3 and 5.4 demonstrate findings from Richardson's analysis employing the same data visualization techniques using data from the three different groups' (A, B, C) average mathematics scores. The two subtests of mathematics performance are 'arithmetic reasoning' and 'arithmetic computation'. Figure 5.4 shows that the English-speaking Coral Way students outperformed the English-speaking non-Coral Way students across both areas (reasoning and computation). For the Spanish-speaking students, the scores are similar to the reading subtests in which the experimental and control group scores are closely aligned. We also do not know the level of statistical significance of these scores. In addition, the scores between the intervention group and match sample group are very similar. This finding from 1968 confirmed that there was no academic loss (in the five subtests) among students who participated in bilingual instruction.

It is important to hypothesize and underscore the intense nature and focus on language development for the Coral Way students. The English and Spanish teachers, as well as the aides, focused intently on building language skills through repetition, drill and vocabulary in both languages.[10] There was strict separation of language during academic content areas, and teachers had time to plan and ensure that the curriculum was aligned in Spanish and in English. If the unstated mission of Coral Way was to prove that two-language instruction would not have a negative effect on learning, the data show that the Coral Way mission was accomplished.

Goal Numbers 3–7: Culture, Community, Vocation and Social Contributions

Teachers, students and parents

Social experiments have important qualitative components that are not measured using quantitative data following statistical analyses, yet they yield important insights into other outcomes. Some of the early goals of Coral Way addressed the satisfaction of students and their subsequent contributions to the community and to society. Other qualitative measures in social experiments of education can include teacher satisfaction and parental or caregiver satisfaction of a particular program or intervention. Here, we can glean important information pointing toward student engagement in learning, memories about their educational program, how participants perceived the program and the program's impact on their lives in the long term.

In these areas, Coral Way was undoubtedly a tremendous success. Although there are the limited achievement and language ability data noted previously, there is ample evidence to demonstrate student engagement, positive student perceptions and strong parental satisfaction with the program. Connie Loveland captures this sentiment in her 1966 English paper at the University of Miami, in which she describes Coral Way Elementary as 'helping to produce more tolerant and capable citizens for the city of Miami, Florida. In a world as small as ours is, bilingual citizens are invaluable'.[11]

Some of the positive energy surrounding Coral Way can be attributed to its unique status as a pioneering educational program, and a spirit of growth and optimism. Teachers, administrators and bilingual aides felt that their contributions, commitment and hard work would lead to positive social outcomes from the program. Cuban aide Piñeiro recalled the initial uncertainty of the school on the implementation of the bilingual program, 'We [didn't] know exactly how this program [was] going to be', but strong leadership and teacher and staff enthusiasm to take up the challenge of the first two-way bilingual program contributed to the momentum. The 'eagerness of our principal, Mr. Joseph Lee Logan', according to Piñeiro, was a key factor.[12]

Rosaura Sotolongo was hired as a teacher in Coral Way in 1967, four years after the bilingual experiment began. She recalled firmly believing in the program and children's ability to be taught in and to learn two languages. She attributed the success of the program to 'our effort, hard work, patience, and commitment'. Sotolongo referred back fondly to her time at the school as a 'noble journey, filled with incredible adventures for so many years'.[13]

The environment of the school was welcoming and affirming of the Cuban children. Two languages were regularly heard throughout the building, English and Spanish. Loveland's 1966 description noted the high bilingual abilities of the students and her difficulty discerning an accent – in Spanish or English – in the students' speech. For the Cuban-background children, this was a welcoming sound and an affirmation of their linguistic and cultural identities. Looking back, however, for children such as Bess de Farber who were not Cuban, there was sense of not fully belonging culturally. She did sense linguistic affirmation because Spanish was the language her Argentinean mother spoke with Bess and her younger brother at home.

Sotolongo also recalled a bilingual environment where not only were students using two languages, but they were also integrated well during the middle of the school day, especially during unstructured times such as supervised play. She recalled that 'They were children, and they all got together, and especially they played together. And when they talk[ed] in the cafeteria, they [sat] together too'.

Many of the students in the first classes of the school neither realized the unique environment of Coral Way, nor that they were part of a bilingual education experiment. Catherina Poerschke, who began the program in second grade, transferred into the school from Silver Bluff Elementary. Her mother knew Principal Logan personally and insisted on enrolling her daughter. 'Spanish was not spoken in my home', she recalled, 'but my mother knew Mr. Logan, the principal at Coral Way Elementary, and

I don't know how long she had been trying to get me into Coral Way, but I guess it was for some time. She wanted me enrolled in the bilingual program. Evidently Mom knew all about it, and so finally she was able to get me in'.[14] Poerschke attended Coral Way from second through sixth grade. Her fondest memories of school included the friendships she developed: 'We all got along really well. We all intermingled, because actually, to tell you the truth, I think most of my friends that I developed close relationships with, were Spanish'.

Orestes Gonzalez described similar memories: 'I don't know if I'm coloring [my memories] with nostalgia, but everybody seemed pretty happy, in spite of the fact of the trauma of having to leave Cuba and what was happening in Cuba at the time. The school environment was very happy and positive and very healthy. We didn't have a sense of "us" versus "them"'.[15]

Rebecca Porto began the program in 1966 in the fourth grade. She landed in the Coral Way neighborhood by chance, after her parents relocated from another area of Miami. Looking back, Porto describes her time transitioning into the US school system: 'Basically having come from Cuba, not speaking any English, I was thrown into a class where I didn't understand anything that was going on, and it was very traumatic. And then once I got to Coral Way, I was like, "Wow! This is great!" It was wonderful'.[16]

The relationships that teachers built with the students were impressive. The school operated more like a family with caregiver teachers than an institution. Bess de Farber explains the summer between first and second grades. Her teacher, Mrs Richardson, traveled to Europe and painstakingly sent each student a handwritten letter describing her trip to them, looking forward to seeing them the following September. The students reciprocated. Most of the Spanish-speaking students had never seen snow. During winter holidays, students sent their teachers pictures of their vacations, sharing their newfound experiences.

Although many of the former Coral Way students' parents have passed away, like Bess de Farber's mother when Bess was only 28, they recall their parents' support for the program and the outcomes that they witnessed as a result. Gonzalez reminisces, 'my mother verbalized how happy she was that we were able to be in a class where Spanish was spoken also, but we didn't think it was unusual'.[17]

Like Diana Morales, who earlier described the success she experienced having gone through Coral Way and developed high levels of literacy in both languages, Tatiana Palma's family relocated from the northeast United States to Miami in 1968, in the middle of the school year. Palma was in sixth grade and attended Coral Way for only six

Image 5.1 Coral Way student during winter vacation

months. She recalls her parents, now deceased, and the family's move to Miami, 'for all I knew, I would learn more Spanish, which they were thrilled about, because Spanish, of course, was our language at home. But I didn't know how to write it, and I didn't know how to read it. And so my parents felt very strongly, my mother in particular, that it would be a wonderful plus for me educationally and culturally'.[18]

Cross-cultural outcomes and the advantages of having cultural understandings across groups are difficult to capture, particularly in the long term. Yet biculturalism,[19] or the ability to feel comfortable in two cultures, was always a primary goal of the Coral Way experience and a stated goal of the experiment. Mackey and Beebe's (1977: 81) review of the Coral Way model, following the limited data derived from Richardson's 1968 dissertation, readily acknowledged that 'students at Coral Way Elementary were learning to operate effectively in two languages and two cultures… being prepared to live satisfying lives and to contribute to their bicultural community and country'. Those findings, supported by the relationship between the Coral Way school and the surrounding community, were key outcomes of the experiment.

Gladys Margarita Diaz described earlier the cross-cultural understanding she learned through the curriculum, where teachers taught a 'pan-Hispanic' view of what it meant to be bicultural. She continued, however, to note that the curriculum was more than a reading activity:

those cultures [were] real to the students, so that they have reality on what their culture is, like if you're from Guatemala or you're from Ecuador or you're from Colombia, what is the history of your culture? So that the kid isn't embarrassed to be Hispanic, it's something to be proud of.[20]

Leticia Lopez recalled that Cubans represented the majority of Hispanics at the school, with some students from Guatemala and Colombia. In other words, the identity of the Cuban students at Coral Way was affirmed as part of a bigger, pan-Hispanic identity, and something that the Spanish-speaking teachers aimed for students to understand through Spanish art during the renaissance, knowledge of various linguistic forms of Spanish or the histories of countries such as Ecuador, Venezuela and Colombia.

Long-Term Social Outcomes

The earliest goals of Coral Way were to build, foster and affirm students' bilingualism; assist their integration into society; and support positive social and vocational outcomes. This is a surprising set of goals, because the Cuban students and teachers felt that their stay in the United States was temporary, at least initially and for the years 1963–1968. Perhaps this is why there were no measures of student or parent satisfaction, nor a plan to follow students over a longer period of time. Despite that limitation, the design of the bilingual education experiment was predicated upon long-term positive outcomes for students, including added socioeconomic and vocational benefits for students and the students' contributions to society. In other words, the early visionaries of Coral Way did indeed want students to have access to social and economic capital as a result of the program.

Although the 1960s in the United States ushered in the civil rights movement, which affected schooling and education through legislated racial desegregation, there is no mention in school documents, interviews or media sources that the school aimed for educational equity in the sense of students having a language right to learn through the medium of their home language. At the same time, the Coral Way leaders did not see language as a problem but rather as a resource for learning academic content. But, outside of the early pressure to register the large number of Cuban students and to communicate with them, Spanish for the Cuban students was also not viewed as a problem. What the experiment did, however, was demonstrate that students first languages could be used as a resource for learning academic content in a second language, with no loss to the first.

Among the oral histories conducted with former students of Coral Way who attended in the early years of the program, is Gladys Margarita. The impact of the Coral Way bilingual education program had a lasting effect. Her story exemplifies those of students who attended and benefitted from the program. She describes how the Coral Way experience, the development of bilingualism, biliteracy and cross-cultural dexterity, affected her life and identity:

> I think that being that kind of [bilingual and bicultural] person enabled me to be very sure of myself for the rest of my life. When I got to Cornell I lived at the International Living Center. My best friends were from Colombia and Venezuela and Argentina, and my Spanish got really, really good... And then as a result, I wound up being much more dexterous in commercial and sort of business Spanish.[21]

Gladys continued on to a very successful career, which she attributes to the Coral Way bilingual program:

> ... I got my securities license in 1985, which is the National Association of Securities Dealers Series VII license. I was probably one of the first Hispanic women that took that exam in the mid-eighties. I went to work for a company called Bear-Stearns and Company. Bear-Stearns is one of the largest trading firms in the world. They didn't have anyone to cover the Latin America desk, and so I was assigned to the international department for *only one reason* – I could speak Spanish fluently, I was an Ivy League graduate, and I had my securities license. If I had not had the basics of Coral Way Elementary, my love of language and my love of literature in Spanish, I wouldn't have been able to hit that mark.[22]

Rebecca Porto, who attended Coral Way from 1966 to 1968, found herself at the school when her family moved into the neighborhood. She described the identity affirmation that she experienced at the school, 'It validated my identity. I think that was very important. If I hadn't been in that program, maybe I would have forgotten where I came from, and tried to be 100% American'. Tatiana Palma describes her identity as 'I always identified much, much more with American culture. And I think that was really a selective choice on my part'. Perhaps the words of Bess de Farber most aptly sum up the outcomes of Coral Way and its impact on individual lives, 'I feel that it saved my Spanish-speaking life from being nonexistent, or being only existent with my mother. I can read and write it, and I understand it, and I'm just a more complete person than I would have been, had I just been in an American school'.

The Coral Way experiment was much more than an experiment in language and literacy development among two different groups of students. It aimed to ensure that students learned about history across Latin American and Spain and had a broad understanding of cross-cultural communication; that they developed identities that were affirmed as

Cubans, Americans and bilinguals; that they benefitted from their bilingualism vocationally and economically; and that, ultimately, as they matured, they had the power to *construct* identities.

In a later report on Coral Way, Dr Pauline Rojas (1965: 237) summarized the ultimate goal of the program, 'The over-all objective in the education of the bilingual child is his integration into the main stream of American life'. She continues that, 'he [sic] must be so educated that that he will be able to operate in English when the situation demands English and operate in his own language when the situation demands the use of his own language'. With respect to teaching bilingual children, Rojas, then still the director of the Office of Bilingual Education for Dade County Public Schools, focused on the Spanish speakers' language development and social and cultural integration into mainstream society.

What we can say about the Coral Way 'ultimate' goal is that the children who participated did demonstrate a strong command of English and Spanish, literacy in both languages and were seemingly well adjusted. We also know that many of the children who attended Coral Way were adept at navigating the broader bilingual and bicultural community, and conveyed a strong sense of identity, affirmation, cultural dexterity and social integration. None who remained in the program and who were interviewed in the early archives at the University of Arizona or in the subsequent archives or at the University of Florida stated that the bilingual education program failed to foster bilingualism, biliteracy or social integration (Rojas, 1965).

Notes

(1)   Rojas, P. and Robinett, R. (1963, October 29) A report: Progress report on Ford Foundation Projects. University of Florida Digital Collections. See https://ufdc.ufl.edu/AA00066059/00001.

(2)   Richardson, M.W. (1964, May 14) A study of certain aspects of the achievement of Coral Way Elementary pupils in the bilingual program. Unpublished project proposal. University of Florida Digital Collections. See https://ufdc.ufl.edu/AA00066042/00001.

(3)   Richardson, M.W. (1968, January) An evaluation of certain aspects of the academic achievement of elementary pupils in a bilingual program. Unpublished doctoral dissertation. University of Miami. University of Florida Digital Collections. See https://ufdc.ufl.edu/AA00067747/00001.

(4)   See note 3, p. 41.

(5)   Manuel, H.T. (1963) Tests of General Ability and Reading. Inter-American Series. University of Texas, Austin. ERIC Document ED003857.

(6)   Feinberg, R.C. (2019) Personal communication on Coral Way.

(7)   See note 3, p. 37.

(8)   N.A. (1964, April 29) Hall reports on bilingual school (p. 27). *Miami Herald*.

(9)   N. A. (1964, August 16) Spanish 'crisis' is lessening (p. 157). *Miami Herald*.

(10) de Farber, B. (2018, November 29) Interview by M.R. Coady [audio file]. Coral Way Elementary. University of Florida Digital Collections.

(11) Loveland, C.L. (1966, December 9) Coral Way Elementary: A Bilingual School. University of Florida Digital Collections. See https://ufdc.ufl.edu/AA00066052/00001.

(12) Piñeiro, M. (2008, June 21). Interview by B. de Farber [Audio file]. Coral Way Elementary. University of Florida Digital Collections. Retrieved from https://ufdc.ufl.edu/AA00065593/00001.

(13) Sotolongo, R. (2008 March 13). Interview by R. Ruiz. [Audio file]. Coral Way Elementary. University of Florida Digital Collections. Retrieved from https://ufdc.ufl.edu/AA00065589/00001/.

(14) Poerschke, C.F. (2008, March 14) Interview by R. Ruiz [audio file]. Coral Way Elementary. University of Florida Digital Collections. See https://ufdc.ufl.edu/AA00065592/00001.

(15) Gonzalez, O. (2008, March 26) Interview by R. Ruiz [audio file]. Coral Way Elementary. University of Florida Digital Collections. See https://ufdc.ufl.edu/AA00065599/00001.

(16) Porto, R. (2008, March 14) Interview by R. Ruiz [audio file]. Coral Way Elementary. University of Florida Digital Collections. See https://ufdc.ufl.edu/AA00065591/00001?search=porto.

(17) de Farber, B. (2018, November 29) Interview by M.R. Coady [audio file]. Coral Way Elementary. University of Florida Digital Collections.

(18) Palma, T. (2008, March 15). Interview by R. Ruiz [Audio file]. Coral Way Elementary. University of Florida Digital Collections. Retrieved from https://ufdc.ufl.edu/AA00065595/00001.

(19) Rosa Guas Inclán (1972) describes Coral Way's biculturalism as simply 'culturalism'. She argues that Coral Way students become adept at navigating multiple cultures and cross-culturally.

(20) Diaz, G.M. and Diaz, J.G. (2008, March 15) Interview by R. Ruiz [audio file]. Coral Way Elementary. University of Florida Digital Collections. See https://ufdc.ufl.edu/AA00065600/00001.

(21) See note 17.

(22) See note 17.

References

Bell, P.W. (1969) Bilingual education in an American elementary school. In H.H. Stern (ed.) *Languages and the Young School Child* (pp. 112–118). London: Oxford University Press.

Chall, J.S. (1983) *Stages of Reading Development*. New York: McGraw Hill.

Kitson, L. (2011) Tween here and there, transitioning from the early years to the middle years: Exploring continuities and discontinuities in a multi-literate environment. *Literacy Learning: The Middle Years* 19 (1), 9–17.

Mackey, W.F. and Beebe, V.N. (1977) *Bilingual Schools for a Bicultural Community: Miami's Adaptation to the Cuban Refugees*. Rowley, MA: Newbury House.

Møller, J.S., Jørgensen, J.N. and Holmen, A. (2014) Polylingual development among Turkish speakers in a Danish primary school: A critical view on the fourth grade slump. *International Journal of Bilingual Education and Bilingualism* 17 (1), 32–54.

Richardson, M. (1968) An evaluation of certain aspects of the academic achievement of elementary pupils in a bilingual program. Unpublished doctoral dissertation, University of Miami.

Rojas, P. (1965) Instructional materials and aids to facilitate teaching the bilingual child. *The Modern Language Journal* 49 (4), 237–239.

Zentella, A.C. (1990) Linguistic leveling in four New York City Spanish dialects: Linguistic and social factors. *Hispania* 73 (4), 1094–1105.

6 The Building of a Bilingual Network

How the community functioned around the Coral Way neighborhood, and their attitudes toward children from Cuba, especially those arriving under Operation Pedro Pan, impacted the positive reception that Spanish-speaking students received. However, not everyone saw the benefits of bilingualism, nor considered the experiment to have potential positive outcomes.

Dissent

It was not until late 1965 that dissent among parents surfaced to the level of letters to the district superintendent and in the media outlets. Clearly, some parents were concerned enough about the experiment to question, write and protest. For some English-speaking parents, the use of Spanish in their child's education challenged the linguistic rights of their own children, that is, the right to be educated in English only. A late 1965 letter to Superintendent Joe Hall appearing in *The Miami Herald* was written by Mrs Murphy. Murphy states that she is writing on behalf of 'all the parents of the Coral Way Elementary School children', assuring readers that the group was 'not just a handful of hysterical mothers' who were protesting spontaneous and revolutionary programmatic changes at Coral Way. Murphy references television, radio and newspaper articles of the time that questioned the experiment and its possible negative effect on student learning.

The letter proceeds to lament the use of taxpayer dollars paid by parents, who were receiving nothing for their high taxes other than heartache and the use of children as guinea pigs. Murphy describes the Coral Way bilingual program as 'un-American' and 'chaotic' and, ultimately, what Cuban parents wanted: 'proper teachings of what a democratic government really is – so that in the event they are able to return to a free Cuba, these children will have had the best possible foundation of a democratic life'.[1] The next day, Murphy's letter was met with a strong rebuttal by Elaine Porter, the mother of a fourth-grade student, Amy, who, her mother argues was benefitting academically and linguistically from the program.[2]

Murphy's letter signaled a physical and ideological protest against the bilingual education program. In mid-December 1965, a group of protesting parents from Coral Way described their fifth-grade children, who were the few not participating in the Coral Way bilingual program, as 'educational orphans'. The school board assuaged their concerns by promising to identify a solution for their children by the board meeting on 5 January 1966.[3]

Affirmation

Despite the English-only parents' concerns about their children remaining in a bilingual program that did not include them, and their political views that bilingual education was 'un-American', a positive reception continued to permeate the Coral Way neighborhood. Tatiana Palma described the community in family-like terms, where 'parents got to know other parents, and kids got to know each other a little bit better. We went to each other's homes, celebrated each other's birthdays and that kind of thing'. She noted that there was a 'common thread' connecting the families culturally, through the school and into the community.[4] de Farber, whose parents were Argentinian, recalls her father befriending their local postman, who later helped him to purchase a car. The geographic location of her house, which was directly across the street from Coral Way, made her feel that the school was an extension of her home for more than six years.

Piñeiro recalled similarly that Principal Logan frequented a local barbershop where the father of one of the students was employed. She recalled that Logan insisted on the shop because he wanted to practice his Spanish. And Cuban aide Teresita Brito's mother made dresses for Logan's wife. Piñeiro reminisces, 'It was like a close family. We got very, very, very close'.[5] Orestes Gonzalez remembered how the use of Spanish in the school helped to build relationships between parents and teachers, because Spanish was not only used but also welcomed at the school. 'There were no prohibitions', Gonzalez recalls, 'as far as speaking Spanish in the school whatsoever'. Palma, like other former Coral Way graduates noted in this book, attributes her personal accomplishments to the Coral Way community, which was built around the bilingual education program. 'I still am a product of this community', she asserts, 'and have lived here off and on for many years – is pretty tight-knit culturally and socially'. Although the school ensured that a specific language was used for instruction in each segment

Image 6.1 Bessie de Farber in front of Coral Way (c. 1963)

(morning/afternoon), students at Coral Way always felt their languages were not only used, but also welcomed.

The Coral Way school was the epicenter of the community, and it was clear that by the end of the 1964 school year, the experiment had taken off. The teacher professional development project in summer 1963, which was funded by the Ford Foundation and attended by focused and determined teachers and Cuban aides, succeeded in producing materials for teachers in the first year of the experiment. But that work grew more intense in the summer of 1964 with teachers having had a full academic year of experience working with the materials produced in 1963. The complications surrounding the various literacy levels of students and placing them in either the Spanish or English group was a point of discussion and change. In addition, the *Miami Linguistic Readers* were expanded to include more readers and materials. By August 1964, Rojas reported to the *Miami Herald* that 40 out-of-state groups of English as a second language (ESL) children would be using the readers. The non-Florida groups included Mexican-American students in California, Colorado and Texas; native American peoples in Arizona and New Mexico; and Puerto Rican students learning English on the island.[6] By the end of 1966, the number of readers produced by the Ford-funded team was 17 books.[7]

A Second Bilingual Program in Miami

The materials supported a network of educators who were teaching ESL. However, bilingual network building was another matter. Despite the concern by some English-speaking families in the area that the Coral Way experiment was creating 'educational orphans',[8] a second bilingual education program was proposed for Dade County schools. The selected school was Central Beach Elementary School, approved by the Dade school board on 4 May 1966, which aimed to open grades K–3 – four grades – simultaneously. Superintendent Joe Hall offered alternative English-only programs at North Beach or South Beach Elementary schools to dissenting parents and school board member Holmes Braddock. Both alternative schools were located within two miles of Central Beach Elementary.

Similar to prior concerns expressed by the community, the school board signaled that the second bilingual program at Central Elementary would not cost taxpayers additional money, and the only new staffing would be three certified Spanish-speaking teachers. What was not discussed publicly were any additional testing materials or assessments that would be needed to assess students' performance in English and in Spanish, nor teacher education, curriculum and materials. In other words, the public was repeatedly assured, both at the start of the Coral Way experiment and the expansion of this model to Central Elementary, that the cost of implementing the two-way program would be minimal.

Bilingual Programs and Visitors

In addition to expanding into the surrounding Miami communities and nationally, the school gained international attention. In fact, as soon as the program opened its doors, visitors came to Coral Way to sit in classes, observe teaching instruction and learn about the organization of students and language. Principal Logan and his staff maintained documents of visitors, both from the United States and abroad, in their files. In 1966, for instance, two Guatemalan visitors completed applications to enter the United States to visit Coral Way. One was Luis Morales Chúa, editor of the newspaper *Prensa Libre* in Guatemala City. He was accompanied by Manuel Eduardo Rodríguez, editor of the newspaper *El Imparcial* in Guatemala City. On their applications were the two men's current employment, biographical data including their knowledge of English, educational background and family members. Morales, who was a founding member of the Operación Escuela Committee, applied for permission to the US state department to visit Coral Way to learn how Guatemalan education could be improved.

Other visitors included the assistant superintendent of New York City schools, Rose Schwab; Paul Kolers from the Massachusetts Institute of Technology; and Miccosukee school teacher Miss Wallace in 1964. Annelies Hoppe, the German Senator for Education visited in 1965, and in 1967, visitors from Puerto Rico's Department of Public Education, seeking innovative ESL teaching methods, commented on Coral Way's quality use of cooperative teaching, co-planning among teachers and use of audiovisual aids in instruction.[9] Sánchez recalled minsters of education from South Africa and France sitting at the back of her classroom.

Within a short period of time, the Coral Way bilingual program had contributed to a growing and powerful network of bilingual educational programs across the United States. This occurred through the piloting and use of the *Miami Linguistic Readers*, and observations of the school and teacher instruction by international dignitaries, other teachers and the international press. In addition, Rojas, Bell and other scholars such as Gaardner and Inclán began to write about the bilingual education program and its effect on student learning. Although few data on student learning have actually been reported from the initial groups of students, observational data are referenced by the leaders and by Dade County administrators. Bell (1969: 118), for instance, wrote about the students 'rapidly becoming bilinguals who are distinctly "culturally advantaged"... and being prepared to live satisfying lives'.

As I have noted in this book, language ideologies are intertwined with bilingual education, and those in turn are constructed in a broader social and political context. It is not a coincidence that Coral Way as a bilingual two-way immersion program emerged during the height of the civil rights movement in the United States. President Lyndon Johnson signed the Civil Rights Act on 2 July 1964. The sociopolitical context was ripe for advocating for first language instruction in the United States. Scholars of bilingual education such as Tony Baez, Kathy Escamilla, María Fránquiz, Ofelia García and others have written about the contribution, leadership, advocacy and political stance of the early educators of bilingual education that fortified the movement and, arguably, culminated with the passing of the Bilingual Education Act in 1968. These scholars and *antepasados* did not stop there. They continued to build a bilingual education network of academics with government funding under Title VII of the Elementary and Secondary Education Act and remained socially and politically active. This is necessary in building a network of bilingual educators and advocates locally, nationally and internationally.

Graduates of the Coral Way Bilingual Program

Beyond their elementary school experience, many of the Coral Way graduates flourished. The Ford Foundation continued to shape educational policies in the United States, well into higher education with targeted funding for education. Scholars describe the foundation as 'one of the most influential shapers of higher education, domestically and globally' in the 1960s and 1970s (MacDonald & Hoffman, 2012: 253). The Ford Foundation's financial support of Dade County's first public bilingual school, Coral Way, was made under a general special programs fund, which was subsequently redirected to ethnic group studies across the United States. It is not coincidental that the Ford Foundation expanded into higher education about the same time that teachers of Coral Way obtained advanced degrees. In other words, financial support for bilingual education came through specific and earmarked channels from private organizations. Sánchez describes the subsequent bilingual teachers who were funded to study at the University of Miami.[10] Cuban teachers, then, became fully credentialed bilingual educators with state certification and degrees in addition to those they already obtained in Cuba.

Students benefitted from the ongoing professional development of the teachers, noted in Chapter 3 on teacher education. They also benefitted from resources that the teachers stated they received: daily planning time and a community environment and support for the program. However, above all, the students in Coral Way – those from both the Spanish-speaking and the English-speaking sides of the program – state that the relationships they built with teachers and teachers' high expectations for their learning, were paramount.

Diana Morales graduated from Coral Way after entering the school in the fourth grade in 1971. The affirming and supporting bilingual experience at Coral Way inspired Diana to continue her education as a bilingual educator. She describes the Coral Way experience as 'absolutely' transforming her life. Her biliteracy development was essential to her life decisions as a veteran teacher and school psychologist, working with the Florida Inclusion Network, a Florida Department of Education discretionary agency that provides support for students with special learning needs. Diana states that Coral Way 'opened doors', not only for her but also for her daughter in Boston who became a bilingual teacher in an East Boston school.[11]

Orestes Gonzalez, so moved and changed by his affirming bilingual experience as a Cuban, continued his degree in architecture in Texas and gravitated toward art and photography and is a voice for Cuban culture and experience. Gonzalez (2017) authored *Julio's House*. In this book, Gonzalez describes his uncle's flamboyant and uniquely Cuban-Liberace decorating style, which remained hidden in his uncle's modest Miami home. Using photographic images, Gonzalez (2019) draws a link between his uncle's social life as a gay man and the social space he created as he transitioned between life in Cuba and life in the United States.

Image 6.2 Diana Morales in front of Coral Way (2018)

He attributes Coral Way as being a formative part of his identity and influence on his childhood, noting

> nostalgia kind of clouds the things you remember... what's really funny about Coral Way is you're almost like wearing a bubble in the sense that I was Cuban and being Cuban I was surrounded by other Cubans... being in a place where you didn't feel different was very important.[12]

Networks of bilingual education extended from the personal to the local to the international level. The graduates of the first two-way bilingual education program in the United States were the most likely advocates of bilingual education. Many of them continued to promote bilingualism and biliteracy among their own children and to work in vocations where they not only used their own language and literacy skills but also supported others to do so as well. Like Margarita Gladys and Leti Lopez, they worked, studied and traveled internationally.

Yet, the benefits of bilingualism, biliteracy and cross-cultural communication extended to both the Spanish- and English-speaking students. Amy Porter was a student at Coral Way in 1963 when she entered second grade in the bilingual program. She attended Coral Way for five school years until sixth grade and subsequently went on to secondary schools in

Miami, eventually ending up at Wellesley College, where she majored in French. When asked about the long-term goals of the Coral Way bilingual experiment, such as gaining cultural competence and being receptive to people from other cultures, she agrees without hesitation. Amy, who works in business near the bustling Champs Élysées in Paris, France, states, 'As I continued my schooling, the fact that I had been exposed to another culture and to another language had a definite effect on my view of the world. I consider myself to be someone who's very open to other cultures'. As to the economic benefits of bilingualism, Amy describes being 'specifically hired for my multilingual capacity'.[13]

Perhaps most insightful in examining the implications of the Coral Way experiment are the voices of the students who attended and the parents who took a leap of faith and participated in the program. The voices of students from this study demonstrate without a doubt that many of the Coral Way students who attended between 1963 and 1968 from the Spanish- and English-speaking sides of the program, did, indeed, find fulfilling careers that were built on the bilingual networks that they established into adulthood. They used their bilingualism, biliteracy and cultural knowledge, generally speaking, to their advantage and had prosperous employment. The students – now adults – held vivid and fond memories of their time at Coral Way. Teachers felt like family, and the Coral Way students continued to build bilingualism and to promote biliteracy for their own children and grandchildren for generations to come.

Notes

(1) Murphy, N. (1965, November 28) Letter to Dr Joseph Hall. *Miami Herald* (p. 18–E). UF Digital Collections. See https://ufdc.ufl.edu/AA00066090/00001.

(2) Porter, I.W. (1965, November 29) Letter to Dr Joe Hall. UF Digital Collections. See https://ufdc.ufl.edu/AA00066074/00001.

(3) Mann, P. (1965, December 16) Board caught in middle of parents' school battles. *Miami Herald*. UF Digital Collections. See https://ufdc.ufl.edu/AA00066091/00001.

(4) Palma, T. (2008, March 15) Interview by R. Ruiz [audio file]. Coral Way Elementary. University of Florida Digital Collections. See https://ufdc.ufl.edu/AA00065595/00001.

(5) Piñeiro, M. (2008, June 21) Interview by B. de Farber [audio file]. Coral Way Elementary. University of Florida Digital Collections. See https://ufdc.ufl.edu/AA00065593/00001.

(6) N.A. (1964, August 16) Spanish 'crisis' is lessening (p. 157). *Miami Herald*.

(7) Antevil, J. (1966, June 26) Bilingual program of Dade Schools will get award (p. 7). *Miami Herald*.

(8) See note 3.

(9) There are 13 formal letters in the UF Digital Collections from various visitors of the school to Mr J.L. Logan. The letters are dated between February 1964 and April 1967. Mr Logan also kept lists of names of visitors. Some examples follow:

Government Affairs Institute (1966) Biographies of two participants in the 1966 International Visitor Program of the US Department of State. University of Florida Digital Collections. See https://ufdc.ufl.edu/AA00066048/00001.

Hoppe, A. (1965, April 2) Letter to J.L. Logan. University of Florida Digital Collections. See https://ufdc.ufl.edu/AA00065950/00001.

Hoppe, A. (1965, May 31) Letter to J.L. Logan. University of Florida Digital Collections. See https://ufdc.ufl.edu/AA00065953/00001.

Persky, B. (1964, November 6) Letter to J.L. Logan. University of Florida Digital Collections. See https://ufdc.ufl.edu/AA00065961/00001.

Weed, A.P. (1965, May 9) Letter to J.L. Logan. University of Florida Digital Collections. See https://ufdc.ufl.edu/AA00065960/00001.

(10) Sánchez-Pando, J. (2008, March 13) Interview by R. Ruiz [audio file]. Coral Way Elementary. University of Florida Digital Collections. See http://ufdc.ufl.edu/AA00065594/00001.

(11) Morales, D. (2018, October 13) Interview by M.R. Coady [audio file]. Coral Way Elementary. University of Florida Digital Collections.

(12) Gonzalez, O. (2008, March 26) Interview by R. Ruiz [audio file]. Coral Way Elementary. University of Florida Digital Collections. See https://ufdc.ufl.edu/AA00065599/00001.

(13) Porter, A. (2019, June 3) Interview by M.R. Coady [audio file]. Coral Way Elementary. University of Florida Digital Collections.

References

Bell, P.W. (1969) Bilingual education in an American elementary school. In H.H. Stern (ed.) *Languages and the Young School Child* (pp. 112–118). London: Oxford University Press.

MacDonald, V. and Hoffman, B.P. (2012) 'Compromising *La Causa?*': The Ford Foundation and Chicano intellectual nationalism in the creation of Chicano history, 1963–1977. *History of Education Quarterly* 52 (2), 251–281.

Gonzalez, O. (2017) *Julio's House*. New York: Kris Graves Projects and Canada: Quadriscan.

Gonzalez, O. (2019) *Orestes Gonzalez*. Retrieved from https://www.orestesgonzalez.com/.

Epilogue

The establishment of Coral Way as the earliest two-way immersion bilingual education program with native English- and native Spanish-speaking students was, indeed, a social experiment, and its outcome was uncertain at the time of its inception. By now it is apparent that a multitude of factors – sociopolitical, economic, ideological and experiential – converged in those early years, precipitating the development of the program and allowing it to take place. Even though the visionaries described in this book, Dr Pauline Rojas, Paul Bell, Ralph Robinett, J. Lee Logan and Dr Mabel Richardson, to name a few, had limited measures of achievement and no measures immediately aligned to students' social integration, vocation and cross-cultural abilities, there is ample evidence to suggest that in those areas, the program was successful for many students but especially for those from Spanish-speaking backgrounds. Nonetheless, students such as Bess de Farber, who felt that their identities were not fully reflected in the curriculum, and who were placed into linguistic groups based on the sound of their last name, fondly recalled the teachers and community surrounding Coral Way.

Revisiting the Sociopolitical Context of Coral Way

In the years following the 1963 start of Coral Way as a two-way immersion program, the US government began to officially and financially support bilingual education programs in areas across the United States through federal policies, the most important of which was the 1968 Bilingual Education Act (BEA). The Act was introduced by the progressive democratic senator from Texas, Ralph Yarborough, and passed by Congress in 1967, only a few short years after the Coral Way bilingual program started and a year before Richardson published her quantitative findings on bilingual student learning. There is reason to believe, though, that Richardson released those findings to officials before completing her final dissertation work.[1] Chicano rights, farmworker rights and the US civil rights movements generated powerful social momentum. Undoubtedly, the social momentum and political activism of the time contributed to the passing of the Act.

Ruiz (1983) examined the context in which the BEA was passed. In 1983, shortly before his widely cited 1984 article on language planning – language as problem, right, resource – Ruiz described that 'the original version of Title VII in 1967 specified not only a non-English primary language but also poverty (that is, less than $3,000 income per year per family) as eligibility criteria...' (Hornberger, 2016, loc. 6532). Ruiz argued that both non-English language ability and poverty were already conceptualized as language ideology in the American psyche at that time. In the social and political context of Coral Way in 1963, these two demographic characteristics of non-English ability and poverty were also likely factors in establishing the program. However, poverty among the early Cuban refugees was, for many, the result of not being able to bring financial resources or professional credentials with them from Cuba.

The civil rights and social movements stimulated bilingual education programs in other regions of Florida and other parts of the United States (Ovando, 2003).

Ovando (2003: 7) describes this era of progressive language policies and programs as the 'opportunistic period'. Locally in the Miami area, there was a general feeling of altruism toward Cuban refugees, particularly children left without parents and families, who were principally housed in makeshift orphanages or 'temporary shelters' like Camp Matecumbe in the Miami area. The last camp for children did not officially close until 1981 (Conde, 1999). Stepick and Stepick (2009) describe the programs, policies and services that were afforded Cubans refugees in the area as opposed to the dearth of those social programs for other groups. Those factors undeniably contributed to the Coral Way bilingual program.

As the saying goes, the start of the Coral Way bilingual program was not all a bed of roses. Dissenting voices contesting the value of bilingualism appeared on the national scene. Ovando (2003) cites Noel Epstein as one naysayer who viewed bilingual education and its national expansion as a 'death wish' on the United States, because it would separate linguistic groups and threaten American unity. Is it truly 'un-American' to speak, use, read and write more than one language? As data from the Coral Way bilingual program revealed, once English-speaking parents experienced the bilingual benefits of the program and, later, outperformed students in monolingual settings, more of them sought to enroll their children in the program than those who wanted to withdraw them.

English-speaking children who graduated from Coral Way continued to experience the benefits of bilingualism, and many continued to view bilingualism as an asset for their own children.

Contrary to Epstein's view regarding the relationship between national identity and a single, unifying language, it is clear that the United States has never been a single language nation, nor has bilingual education been absent from the earliest educational programs that existed even before Coral Way as a two-way program. As noted throughout this book, language ideologies are intertwined with bilingual education. Despite more than 200 years of nationhood and multilingualism, the United States today is not at risk of being socially or politically disunified. In other words, the one-language, one-state ideology is a pervasive myth that continues to permeate the American psyche to a large degree. What people believe about language and its role in US society continues to be examined and debated through movements such as English only or official English, which rely on the monolingual, monocultural myth.

At the local level, none of the students who graduated from the Coral Way bilingual program was decidedly un-American in their self-view. American culture – or at least some aspect of what that meant in the 1960s – was embedded in the curriculum, especially music, literature and patriotic songs. But Cuban culture, pan-Latin American histories and the Spanish renaissance were taught right alongside it. Despite those foci on various cultures and students' acquisition of two languages, the graduates of Coral Way today state that they feel as American, if not more so, than any given student in a monolingual school. In fact, the development of bilingualism and biliteracy *was* the galvanizing force that affirmed students' identities as members of the Coral Way community and fostered a positive and affirming self-view. Moreover, the power of Coral Way students – although admittedly not all of them, as this book has revealed – constructed bilingual identities and use(d) bilingualism as a resource, making contributions to the communities in which they live today. As Richard Ruiz understood, the role of the student in bilingual education is the true goal of public education:

> Language is general, abstract, subject to a somewhat arbitrary normalization; voice is particular and concrete. Language has a life of its own – it exists even when it is suppressed; when voice is suppressed, it is not heard – it does not exist... We should ask, what has happened to student voice? Assuming that students' language has been included in the curriculum, whose voice is heard in it if they are not active participants? (Ruiz, 1991: 219–220)

I argue that our collective ability to be inclusive in our curriculum, teaching and varied histories, where multiple voices and perspectives are offered, shared, interrogated and negotiated is exactly what it means to be American. Our American identity is complex, multifaceted, multiracial, multi-ethnic and multilingual. This is the hallmark of American education in general and of bilingual education in particular.

In examining language ideologies, Ruiz maintained that the power of ideologies resides in the experiences of students, families and communities. When listening to Richard conduct the first set of oral histories from Coral Way in 2007 and 2008, I wondered why his questions to former students gravitated toward their language practices in homes and communities. He asked what their parents spoke at home and which children befriended which, in other words, what were the lived language experiences of the homes and community surrounding Coral Way. Richard's work continued to examine the relationship between language ideologies, language policies and the way that languages were used. In 1995, he wrote that '[s]ince languages live in communities, the common life activities of the community must be the targets of language policies' (Ruiz, 1995: 78). In the case of Coral Way, it seems evident that the community surrounding Coral Way reflected a language ideology of bilingualism, but this was the lived experiences of the children who attended Hebrew school and the incoming Cuban refugees.

Following the opportunistic period of language policy in the United States was a repressive period of language policies at the federal and state levels, described by Ovando (2003: 12) as the 'dismissive period' that began in the 1980s. Coral Way continued to operate as a bilingual two-way program, but the backgrounds of students attending the school became increasingly more diverse, reflecting various trends and patterns in immigration. As I noted in the Prologue of this book, students and families of Coral Way represent multiple Spanish-speaking countries from across Latin America. As society became more socially, linguistically and culturally diverse, so did the Coral Way neighborhood and school. Thus, on the one hand is the growth of two-way immersion programs across the United States as more English monolingual families experience the benefits of the programs, while on the other hand is a persistent dismissive period of language diversity.

The Florida Language Context

By 1988, Florida had passed an official English language amendment to the constitution under ballot Measure 11. Some scholars of Florida's language policy aptly note that the legal amendment has had little practical effect on school districts and the way that education operates in the state.[2] However, over the past two decades, Florida's Department of Education has essentially followed a policy of official English despite the real and widespread linguistic diversity across Florida's 67 school districts. For instance, Florida's plan for the Every Student Succeeds Act (ESSA) was rejected four times in 2017 and 2018 (Mitchell, 2018), because the state argued that its official English status precluded them from offering native language assessments to non-native English-speaking students. In their responses to federal pushback regarding the use of first language assessments, Florida repeatedly referenced constitutional protections, hiding behind its official English status.

Under state rule, Florida school districts must indicate their model(s) of instruction for English language learners (ELL) in their district ELL plans once every three years. Two options include dual language (two-way immersion) and developmental bilingual education.[3,4] However, the state does not provide guidance, preparation, professional development or native language assessments and has taken a laissez-faire approach to bilingual education overall. The official English status of the state cannot help but stunt the growth of bilingual education programs, because educators cannot openly assess, affirm or promote the use of languages other than English in schools. Yet, at the same time, Florida recently passed the Seal of Biliteracy (2018) for biliterate students and recognition of that achievement on their high school diplomas. The state allows individual school districts to determine students' biliteracy and to award the seal.

Findings from the Coral Way Archives

I have learned several important things while undertaking the work on the history of Coral Way as the earliest two-way immersion program. I began to analyze the data from the first 14 oral histories over the course of a summer, initially listening to the audio recordings on my smartphone and then through my car speaker while driving in the steamy Florida summer heat. I listened again to the words of the Coral Way visionaries and leaders at home on my computer, when coding the data, and while identifying the themes that cut across the participants' voices. I listened to the recordings when I typed this book and while reading the subsequent findings of the experiment as they were described by Richardson, Logan and Bell. I also checked my hunches with Bess de Farber, Susana Martín, Lourdes Rovira, Marta Aleida Hernández who worked for Ralph Robinett and Rosie Castro Feinberg. I realized that much more needed to be unearthed. I consulted the *Miami Linguistic Readers*, the Ford Foundation, microfiche from the *Miami Herald*, the Cooperative Inter-American tests and individual authors and scholars whose work added context to the Coral Way bilingual program. Some of the most insightful data derived from the Ford Foundation archives, and I obtained limited district data from Dade County Public Schools (DCPS). Sadly, many of the people who were involved in the early bilingual program have since passed away. This makes capturing the history of the Coral Way bilingual program even more urgent, for once these scholars' and educators' voices have passed, our connection to the stories and history, unless documented, has also passed.

The main motif that emerged from my analysis of the data was the sense of community that was created by the people living in the Coral Way neighborhood when Cuban and Spanish-speaking families arrived with uncertain futures. The community adapted, recreated itself and welcomed and embraced children, families and bilingual school staff before and during the bilingual education program. The sense of family in this work seems synonymous with community. As de Farber later recalled, the school 'just seemed like an extension of where I lived'.[5] This was perhaps a combination of having a neighborhood school, teachers who were focused on the social, emotional and academic welfare of Cuban- and US-born students, and perhaps an idyllic sense of childhood freedom in the 1950s and 1960s when children skipped stones and played hopscotch on the sidewalks.

Beyond that scene of community and family are the contributions of the Spanish-speaking teachers and Cuban aides, whose linguistic expertise and bilingualism was the single most valuable resource of the program. The need for those linguistic resources began with the conceptualization of the two-way immersion program in 1961 by Dr Rojas, into 1962–1963 when bilingual Cuban aides assisted children and parents in registering for school and integrating into classrooms, to long summers of teacher education and curriculum development before and after the bilingual program began. To put it succinctly, bilingualism was the most important resource (García, 2009) contributing to the program's success.

Finally, like so many other successful movements and experiments, the need for a focused visionary leader was essential to Coral Way's development and success. Having read through approximately 900 pages of archival data, I would argue that Dr Pauline Rojas's ability to identify resources (funding, personnel, curriculum, materials, networks), her fidelity to the development of bilingualism and biliteracy and her aptitude to address the internal concerns in DCPS and at the Ford Foundation on the establishment of the program was essential. She built time into the program for educators to collaborate and co-plan. It is quite possible that without Rojas and her team with Robinett and Bell, we might not have the growing number of two-way immersion programs in the United States today.

Coral Way Changes Over Time

Coral Way as an institution has had to adapt to numerous educational changes over its 55-year lifespan. Feinberg (1999) recounts that by 1975 there were 8 two-way bilingual elementary schools in Dade County and 18 at the secondary level that had a bilingual curriculum. A decade later, only four of those programs remained, underscoring the 'dismissive period' of bilingual education described by Ovando (2003). It is worth quoting Feinberg at length to illustrate the political force for and against bilingual education over time, and the hard-fought political battles and threats to Dade County's bilingual programs:

> Almost every year, during the period from 1978 to 1988, there was serious consideration of plans to greatly reduce or eliminate parts of the district's bilingual education program and budgets... Every year the danger was averted through the efforts of ad hoc coalitions of community based organizations such as the Spanish American League Against Discrimination (SALAD) and professional organizations such as the Bilingual Association of Florida (the NABE Affiliate in Florida), the Florida Foreign Language Association (FFLA), and Florida Teachers of English to Speakers of Other Languages (Florida TESOL)... The recurring danger was so predictable that a new community-based organization was formed by the teachers in the bilingual program, primarily to better organize resistance efforts. (np)

In other words, ongoing threats to bilingual education were met head-on by organizers, leaders and activists who formed alliances for bilingual students.

Because of those efforts, Coral Way Elementary entered the 21st century as an intact two-way immersion program with as many, if not more, pressures as a monolingual school in Florida and in the United States. Those pressures include incessant testing of students, schools themselves being evaluated with grades, teacher evaluation increasingly aligned to student test scores and a district-wide grading system. Migdania D. Vega, born in Cuba in 1935, was principal of Coral Way Elementary from 1992 to 2003, just before Coral Way expanded from a K-6 school into the Coral Way K-8 Center. Described by teachers and staff during her tenure as 'la diosa', or the goddess,[6] Vega was militant about the teachers' precise use of time, down to the minute, and strict separation of languages for instructional purposes. The biggest challenge that Vega says she faced was the introduction of the school grading system, when schools, like students, were given grades based on performance metrics, many of which involve student standardized test scores. Vega recalled walking the school halls daily, entering classrooms and observing the teachers in order to know 'what was really going on'.[7] She admits being strict with the program but friendly with teachers, sending notes of affirmation and support when she observed good instructional practices. Vega exemplifies the second theme of strong leadership for bilingual education, which is, indeed, a tightrope walk between maintaining the integrity of the bilingual program and adapting to educational trends and change (Palmer, 2018).

Coral Way Elementary became the Coral Way K-8 Center with nearly as much controversy in 2004 as did the initial program in 1963. Local families connected their childhood memories to Coral Way Elementary, having attended the bilingual elementary school and subsequently sending their own children there. They wanted Coral Way to remain a K-6 school. Others saw the expansion of the bilingual program as progressive, offering bilingual children additional opportunities to build biliteracy into their later school grades and to achieve higher language proficiency levels. Susana Martín, for instance, described her husband's desire to hold on to the elementary school model, while she worked at the school during its transition into a K-8 school. The iconic building itself, also needed to transform and expand as the school recreated itself in the early 21st century.

In its most recent configuration, the Coral Way K-8 Center has revised its mission from the initial seven goals of the Ford-funded experimental program to the present time. Today, the mission on the website does not emphasize bilingualism and biliteracy as student learning goals, though the school's external signage remains bilingual and its website welcomes visitors to a bilingual front page. In fact, the school's mission is simply, '[t]o provide the best opportunities for our students in a safe environment' (Coral Way, 2018). Dorner (2014) has identified similar discourses surrounding the establishment of bilingual education programs and similar safety and academic benefits and cultural scripts that are invoked when building these programs. While no one would contest such a mission as important and a necessary objective for student learning, the mission of bilingualism and biliteracy seems absent from today's educational high-stakes pressures and the need to underscore safe schooling.

But as Vega repeatedly acknowledged during our meeting at Luis Galindo's restaurant on a busy Miami street corner, one ongoing problem she faced was ensuring that Spanish was being used and taught with rigor that would lead to high levels of biliteracy. This remains a notable challenge in a state like Florida where there is no systematic, statewide use of Spanish language assessments, including at the Coral Way K-8 Center. Subsequently, there are no standardized Spanish (or other languages) language ability data for educators and scholars to rely on, which would demonstrate areas of need, growth and, most importantly, success among students participating in two-way immersion programs.[8]

I asked Susana Martín if she wanted to know how Coral Way students were performing in Spanish today, relative to other Spanish-learning students in the state and across the United States. She replied yes, but cautioned that teachers already test students in Spanish using the Spanish curriculum series. They use internal data to design, plan and group the students by ability level, which is something that Coral Way teachers in 1963–1968 had to learn to do through trial and error. Like the early Coral Way educators, teachers today also rely on teacher judgment and observations of students as they work in classrooms. The use of teacher knowledge to inform their instructional decisions, Susana feels, allows student groups to be fluid within the classroom and grade levels.[9]

The Spanish language curricular test is administered again at the end of the school year to demonstrate growth in the language and in academic content through Spanish. However, there are no formal, standardized Spanish language assessments other than the College Board Spanish Test that is taken by eighth-grade students at the Coral Way K-8 Center. All formal standardized assessments are those that are state mandated such as the Florida Standards Assessment (FSA), which is only offered in English. When asked if she would like to see how students are performing on standardized assessments of Spanish, Susana replies that it would be interesting to know 'if what we are doing is working in two languages'. But she quickly confesses, 'I don't think teachers would be thrilled to see an additional test'.

State and national guidelines require the use of standardized tests to determine school- and district-level grades, and public bilingual education programs must comply with this mandate. However, students, teachers and schools are held to formal assessments that measure student growth exclusively in English. This is an invalid way of determining student growth and achievement in bilingual education programs, because student learning in the programs occurs over extended periods of time and in two languages (Thomas & Collier, 1997). Simply put, bilingual students function bilingually and need to be assessed bilingually. Without assessing student learning in two languages, as Richardson began to do in 1963, bilingual education programs will continue to be held to a white, monolingual norm (Flores & Rosa, 2015). Bilingual and biliterate students' accomplishments must become a natural, acceptable and integrated part of student, school, district and state performance indicators. This is the least we can do for students who have worked hard and remained committed to the bilingual program, for parents who support the teachers, schools and administrators in the programs and, certainly, for bilingual teachers who dedicate their professional lives to equitable education by advancing bilingualism and biliteracy. This would also assist scholars of bilingual education in regularly informing the public about the positive outcomes of bilingual education and the benefits of bilingualism and biliteracy.

Panning out once more brings into focus the national trends, movements and controversies of bilingual education in general and two-way immersion programs in particular across the United States. What started as the first two-way immersion program at Coral Way has blossomed into more than 2000 programs across the United States today (Center for Applied Linguistics, 2018). Scholars of bilingual education have raised serious questions about the growth of two-way immersion education programs in educating language minoritized students in particular (Valdés, 1997) and issues of equity, when middle-class English-speaking families co-opt programs from language minoritized families. For instance, Valdés, who references Spanish-speaking students in two-way programs with middle-class English speakers, levied three primary concerns regarding dual language: first is the quality of the program when the minoritized language is used in public education; second is the issue of intergroup relations and attending to issues of race between the groups (Flores & Rosa, 2015; Freeman, 1996) and the social status of the languages (English and Spanish); and third is the relationship between language use and power. To this last point, Valdés specifically asks who ultimately benefits from bilingual education programs when increasing numbers of mainstream families realize the added-value of bilingualism and biliteracy?

Although skills in two languages have 'opened doors for members of minority groups... taken to its logical conclusion', Valdés (1997: 419–420) predicted, 'if dual language immersion programs are successful, when there are large numbers of majority persons who are also bilingual, this special advantage will be lost'. Twenty years hence, Valdés's cautionary note remains an equally valid concern today. Scholars continue to study bilingual education programs with intense vigor. For instance, academic debates on bilingual education continue surrounding whether or not languages should be strictly separated in programs. Educators wonder how and under what conditions translanguaging pedagogies will support bilingualism and biliteracy when multilingual students' languages are viewed as a unitary linguistic system (García & Li Wei, 2014). These have important teacher education and pedagogical implications for all educational programs with emerging bilingual students, but especially for bilingual education programs. Other scholars' findings validate Valdés's precautions (Hamman, 2018; Heiman, 2017) and raise new concerns regarding how monoglossic ideologies affect bilingual students' experiences and student learning.

Listening to the Past and Moving into the Future

Challenges in bilingual education

Despite its eminent position as the *abuelita*, or grandmother, of dual-language education, Coral Way is neither beyond current controversies nor outside of similar demographic shifts and neighborhood gentrification trends faced across the United States. Susana Martín recognizes that the stable, middle-class neighborhood that characterized and played a role in the site selection of the first two-way immersion program in the United States continues to undergo demographic changes that will lead to new changes at Coral Way. She predicted that in the near future Coral Way would lose its Title I designation. The Title I designation is a marker of low income among children attending a school or district. Title I schools receive additional federal funding for educating low-income students. The reason for this, she describes, is the rapidly rising cost of housing in the Coral Way neighborhood. She describes a small two-bedroom house located across the street from her own in the Coral Way neighborhood, where the owner's inheritors sold the property. The new owners repaired and updated the house, which sold for nearly double the initial purchase price. Two years later, the house was again listed for sale, at a double-digit percentage price increase. Bess de Farber notes that her father purchased their duplex home in 1961 for about $14,000. Today, Zillow estimates that the home would list on the market for more than $700,000. Few families could afford such a price tag.

Increases in housing costs drive many language minoritized families out of neighborhoods that were once affordable and whose schools relied on the linguistic resources of the children and family to build bilingual education programs. Apple (2006) cautions that neoliberal educational policies, where education is viewed as a commodity and subject to the forces of supply and demand, are powerfully coupled with trends in education that aim to reinstill traditional, neoconservative 'back to basics' values. Two-way immersion programs appear to be one such specialized commodity and equally subject to these larger social motifs that intersect with politics. As Flores and García (2017: 15) describe, the macro-level motifs from which the early two-way immersion programs emerged in the context of civil rights have shifted toward more 'boutique programs' responding to neoliberal paradigms, where parents seek competitive social and economic advantages for their children. This is a caution we must heed. We must carefully understand the relationship between the growth of two-way immersion programs and who benefits from them.

Lessons from Coral Way

Many of the issues faced by the leaders and teachers at Coral Way are faced by educators and scholars today. The path that Coral Way paved allows us to step back in time and examine the origins of the experiment, the unique conditions that led to its development and the key factors that contributed to its success as an educational program model for both monolingual English speakers and for non-native English speakers, both of whom could be considered emergent bilingual students today. The fact that Coral Way continued through periods of intense political pressure to dismantle is testament to the people who continue to organize politically to ensure the future of bilingual education for and on behalf of children from minoritized language backgrounds. In terms of lessons, it is important to harness what we see in the rear-view mirror in order to steer us collectively into a future direction. Like the sentinel sankofa, our historical, sociocultural and familial roots (Rivera & Pedraza, 2000) inform our prediction of what lies before us – the potential roadblocks and the possibilities.

I shared this work with students and colleagues of bilingual education[10] and we discussed and debated the five main findings from the Coral Way bilingual program that directly relate to two-way immersion programs in the United States today. First, Coral Way's teachers were already highly trained teachers in Cuba and were fully invested in the bilingualism and biliteracy development of the children. Funding to provide professional development and teacher credentialing was available and provided to teachers. Today, dual-language two-way immersion programs struggle to find highly trained teachers. Some school districts hire bilingual teachers from Mexico or Spain as one way to ensure that teachers are fully bilingual and biliterate (Dahnke, 2017). But as educators understand, knowing a language is a much different prospect from having the ability to teach it and to teach academic content through it (Shulman, 1987; Turkan et al., 2014). The longer we continue to squander our linguistic resources in Florida and the United States by not offering bilingual education, the more difficult it will be to identify bilingual teachers for bilingual programs.

The second essential factor in Coral Way's success was planning time: having and effectively using planning time for grade-level teams of teachers. Coral Way teachers faithfully used the middle hours of the school day to align the curriculum to student learning and to each other within grade-level teams. The goal of the language switch was to reinforce concepts in the second language that had been taught in the first language. Thus, it was crucial for teachers to plan together. In today's schools there is some debate surrounding bilingual programs not repeating or covering the same material twice (Howard & Sugarman, 2009). Teachers at Coral Way did not sense this stigma. They purposefully repeated content in two languages. Diana Morales referred to this as being 'double dosed' in academic content.[11]

Third, it is clear that the teachers at Coral Way Elementary had a shared mission, namely the bilingual and biliteracy development of all students. They also had tremendous leadership from the district under Dr Pauline Rojas, in the school, from outside funders and the Coral Way community. Leadership matters, especially in the education of bilingual students (Palmer, 2018). Coral Way's leadership was coupled with a sense of creative freedom to continuously refine the program, to adapt student groupings based on the language ability levels of students, which were loosely defined, and to utilize the expertise of Cuban aides to support the mission. The creative freedom and experimental nature of the program allowed for flexibility among the teachers and aides to revise student groups and identify what did and did not work. They worked together as a team. Rather than build creativity and freedom among educators, today's educational climate continues to stifle teachers, limit their ability to network and plan and pigeonhole their work into narrow areas that are relentlessly tested. Incessant testing suffocates creativity, freedom and teachers' work toward a shared mission.

Fourth, there was financial support for the experiment, which allowed visionaries of Coral Way to align teacher expertise, to create materials grounded in a bilingualism-as-resource orientation and to build a favorable context of reception. There was a sense of momentum, of forward thinking and of shared responsibility at Coral Way and within the Coral Way community. As a private organization, the Ford Foundation placed seemingly few restrictions on school district leaders and teachers to create and implement the bilingual program.[12] In stark contrast, today's educational programs are continuously cut financially and are asked to do more with fewer resources and financial incentives. The current pace of educational cutbacks needs to halt and be reversed. It is one thing to be creative with limited resources, but it is another thing to build strong educational programs in the long term without adequate resources.

In addition, a proposed reorganization at the US Department of Education will reduce the visibility and power of the US Office of English Language Acquisition (OELA), formerly known as the Office of Bilingual Education and Minority Languages Affairs (OBEMLA), established in 1974. These name changes reflect national shifts in language ideologies surrounding language minoritized students and bilingual education. The proposed reorganization signals another dilution of bilingual education, where bilingual students are less visible nationally and will likely receive fewer resources. Mitchell (2018) argues that such changes could end in a reduction in services for English learners overall and with few incentives and resources to prepare teachers for bilingual students. If Feinberg's (1999) historical account is at all prophetic, we must remain prepared for the incessant financial reductions, political assaults and social challenges to bilingual programs for the foreseeable future.

Opportunities for bilingual education

Returning to Richard Ruiz's (1984) orientations in language planning, how might we understand the Coral Way experiment between 1961 and 1968 in relation to a language-as-problem, as-right or as-resource orientation, or a combination thereof? The educators of Coral Way demonstrated that bilingualism and multilingual development would not negatively affect learning academic content, and this was a revolutionary finding. Language for the Cuban aides, for Cuban and Spanish-speaking children and for local families in the community was considered a resource, with bilingualism- and multiculturalism-as-resource a stated goal of this revolutionary work. According to the oral histories of Tita Piñeiro and Josefina Sánchez Pando, the surrounding Jewish community supported the language-as-resource ideology, because language and bilingualism were viewed as essential to group identity and economic opportunity. Thus, both the broader social atmosphere and the founders of the Coral Way bilingual program envisioned language as a resource with support for biliteracy development.

What remains surprising is that more than 50 years of research has not convinced politicians or the general public that bilingual education is valuable both in the short and the long term. Krashen (2014: x), who is a frequent author in the call to advance public knowledge and opinion on bilingual education, writes, '[t]hose who oppose bilingual education aim at the media and public and make their work available and comprehensible. We don't do either'. It is not un-American to be multilingual, and I suspect that many of the readers of this book comprise the choir to which we preach. As scholars, we need to use our collective voice, power, knowledge and resources to communicate effectively with mainstream audiences, just as my graduate student noted and described in the Prologue of this book (Machado *et al.*, 2015). For academics, we work within a system that has narrow measures to demonstrate success (e.g. peer-refereed journal articles with impact factors and H indices).[13] Urgent questions we must grapple with include how to align our academic work to mainstream venues and outlets and how to advance and advocate for bilingualism and bilingual education in ways that transform the public and that permeate the public consciousness. We must harness the power of counter-stories in describing educational programs, policies and practices (Golombek *et al.*, 2019), while making those stories accessible to those outside of our field.

I offer several suggestions for scholars and educators involved in language policies, language rights, bilingual education and bilingualism. First is the need for scholars to disseminate their work in mainstream venues to advocate for bilingual education and bilingual students. Making our work accessible is essential to informing the public of the benefits and challenges of bilingual education from US and international perspectives. Second is to partner with journalists and other social media specialists to disseminate and make usable, in language that empowers readers, the findings from educational and social science research. Third is to use film (e.g. Coady, 2013; Kleyn, 2015) and our artistic abilities[14] (e.g. Ada, 2009) to produce visually powerful narratives about bilingual education, multilingual families and communities, and the lived realities of the bilingual experience. These are the lived realities that Richard knew were closely associated with language ideologies and that lead to the possibility of a language-as-resource orientation (Ruiz, 1984, 1995). Most importantly, we need to act cohesively in these areas and as an intellectual community, with urgency, abandon and political awareness.

The courageous vision, determination and transformation that we have experienced and benefitted as a result of the Coral Way educators, leaders and visionaries cannot be lost on us. The momentum from the past must propel us into the future where multilingualism, equity in education and society, diversity and humanizing relationships are our defining hallmark.

Notes

(1) Richardson, M.W. (1968, January) An evaluation of certain aspects of the academic achievement of elementary pupils in a bilingual program. Unpublished doctoral dissertation. University of Miami. University of Florida Digital Collections. See https://ufdc.ufl.edu/AA00067747/00001.
(2) Rosa Castro-Fienberg, personal communication, 2018.
(3) Coady, Bilingual Education in Florida website www.bilingualeducationfl.org (2019).
(4) These options are somewhat ambiguous. When asked, most educators are confused by the model names and types, and there are no options for districts to indicate one-way immersion or other program models. Most bilingual students are placed in 'inclusive' mainstream classrooms, which have had limited effectiveness in Florida (Coady *et al.*, 2016, 2018).
(5) de Farber, B. (2018, November 29) Interview by M.R. Coady [audio file]. Coral Way Elementary. University of Florida Digital Collections.
(6) Martín, S. (2018, October 12) Interview by M.R. Coady [audio file]. Coral Way Elementary. University of Florida Digital Collections.
(7) Vega, M. (2018, October 13) Interview by M.R. Coady [audio file]. Coral Way Elementary. University of Florida Digital Collections.
(8) Some dual-language programs in Florida's Orange County have received private foundation funding to administer the Texas-developed reading assessment, *Tejas Lee* (*Texas Reads*) (http://www.tejaslee.org/).
(9) See note 6.
(10) See especially *Project STELLAR* (https://education.ufl.edu/stellar/) and STELLAR program coordinator Andrew Long, a former dual-language teacher in Florida.
(11) Morales, D. (2018, October 13) Interview by M.R. Coady [audio file]. Coral Way Elementary. University of Florida Digital Collections.
(12) Ford Foundation Digital Archives. *The School Board of Dade County, Florida* (06300064). 17 December 1962 to 16 December 1965.
(13) Referring to academic measures of publications – peer-refereed journals have impact factors and H indices for scholars.
(14) Christian Faltis, for instance, creates culturally responsive, powerful artwork. I asked him if his work was accessible to view online and he replied that it was not.

References

Ada, A.F. (2009) *Vivir en dos idiomas: Memoria*. Doral, FL: Santillana-Aguilar.
Apple, M. (2006) Understanding and interrupting neoliberalism and neoconservatism in education. *Pedagogies: An International Journal* 1 (1), 21–26.
Center for Applied Linguistics (2018) See www.cal.org (accessed 1 December 2018).
Coady, M. (2013) Waiting on DACA. See https://www.youtube.com/watch?v=NDT H1TJZHWo (accessed 1 July 2019).

Coady, M., Harper, C. and de Jong, E. (2016) Aiming for equity: Preparing mainstream teachers for inclusion or inclusive classrooms? *TESOL Quarterly* 50 (2), 340–368. doi: 10.1002/tesq.223

Coady, M., Li, S. and Lopez, M.P. (2018) Twenty-five years after the Florida Consent Decree: Does preparing all teachers work? *FATE Journal* 3 (1), 26–56.

Conde, Y.M. (1999) *Operation Pedro Pan: The Untold Exodus of 14,048 Cuban Children*. New York: Routledge.

Coral Way Bilingual K-8 Center (2018) See https://coralwayk8.wixsite.com/cwk8 (accessed 1 July 2019).

Dahnke, C. (2018) Bilingual teachers, Florida needs you. *Orlando Sentinel*. See https://www.orlandosentinel.com/opinion/os-ed-bilingual-education-florida-teachers-011917-20170120-story.html (accessed 1 July 2019).

Dorner, L.M. (2014) From global jobs to safe spaces: The diverse discourses that sell multilingual schooling in the USA. *Current Issues in Language Planning* 16 (1–2), 114–131.

Feinberg, R.C. (1999) Administration of two-way bilingual elementary schools: Building on strength. *Bilingual Research Journal* 23 (1), 47–68.

Flores, N. and García, O. (2017) A critical review of bilingual education in the United States: From basements and pride to boutiques and profits. *Annual Review of Applied Linguistics* 37, 14–29.

Flores, N. and Rosa, J. (2015) Undoing appropriateness: Raciolinguistic ideologies and language diversity in education. *Harvard Educational Review* 85 (2), 149–171. doi: 10.17763/0017-8055.85.2.149

Freeman, R. (1996) Dual-language planning at Oyster Bilingual School: 'It's much more than language'. *TESOL Quarterly* 30 (3), 557–582.

García, O. (2009) *Bilingual Education in the 21st Century: A Global Perspective*. Malden, MA: John Wiley.

García, O. and Li Wei (2014) *Translanguaging: Language, Bilingualism, and Education*. New York: Palgrave Macmillan.

Golombek, P., Olszewska, A., Marichal, N. and Coady, M. (2019) The Power of Counter-Narratives: Teacher Professional Development. Presentation at the Annual Convention of the National Association for Bilingual Education (NABE), 5–7 March 2019, Orlando, FL.

Hamman, L. (2018) Reframing the language separation debate: Language, identity, and ideology in two-way immersion. Unpublished doctoral dissertation, University of Wisconsin Madison.

Heiman, D. (2017) Two-way immersion, gentrification, and critical pedagogy: Teaching against the neoliberal logic. Unpublished doctoral dissertation, University of Texas at Austin.

Howard, E. and Sugarman, J. (2009) *Program Models and the Language of Initial Literacy in Two-Way Immersion Programs*. Washington, DC: Center for Applied Linguistics. See www.cal.org/twi/literacylanguage.htm (accessed 1 July 2019).

Hornberger, N. (ed.) (2016) *Honoring Richard Ruiz and His Work on Language Planning and Bilingual Education*. Kindle Edition. Bristol: Multilingual Matters.

Kleyn, T. (2015) *Una vida, dos paises*. See http://www.unavidathefilm.com/#introduction-1 (accessed 1 March 2019).

Krashen, S. (2014) Foreword. In G.P. McField (ed.) *The Miseducation of English Learners: A Tale of Three States and Lessons to be Learned* (pp. vii–xiii). Charlotte, NC: Information Age.

Machado-Casas, M., Flores, B.B. and Murillo, E. (2015) Reframing: We are not public intellectuals; we are movement intellectuals. In C. Gerstl-Pepin and C. Reyes (eds) *Reclaiming the Public Dialogue in Education: Putting the Public in Public Intellectual* (pp. 31–38). New York: Peter Lang.

Mitchell, C. (2018, June) If Betsy de Vos scraps the office for ELLs, would it matter? *Education Week*. See https://www.edweek.org/ew/articles/2018/06/20/if-devos-scraps-the-federal-office-for.html (accessed 1 July 2019).

Ovando, C.J. (2003) Bilingual education in the United States: Historical development and current issues. *Bilingual Research Journal* 27 (1), 1–25.

Palmer, D.K. (2018) *Teacher Leadership for Social Change in Bilingual and Bicultural Education*. Bristol: Multilingual Matters.

Rivera, M. and Pedraza, P. (2000) The spirit of transformation. An education reform movement in a New York City Latino/a community. In S. Nieto (ed.) *Puerto Rican Students in US Schools* (pp. 223–243). Mahwah, NJ: Lawrence Erlbaum.

Ruiz, R. (1983) Ethnic group interests and the social good: Law and language in education. In W.A. Van Horne (ed.) *Ethnicity, Law and the Social Good* (pp. 49–73). Milwaukee, WI: University of Wisconsin System.

Ruiz, R. (1984) Orientations in language planning. *NABE Journal* 8 (2), 15–34.

Ruiz, R. (1991) The empowerment of language-minority students. In C.E. Sleeter (ed.) *Empowerment through Multicultural Education* (pp. 217–228). Albany, NY: SUNY Press.

Ruiz, R. (1995) Language planning considerations in indigenous communities. *Bilingual Research Journal* 19 (1), 71–81.

Seal of Biliteracy (2018) State laws regarding the seal of biliteracy. See https://sealofbiliteracy.org/ (accessed 1 March 2019).

Shulman, L.S. (1987) Knowledge and teaching: Foundations of the new reform. *Harvard Educational Review* 57, 1–22.

Stepick, A. and Stepick, C.D. (2009) Diverse contexts of reception and feelings of belonging. *Forum: Qualitative Social Research* 10 (3), Art 15. (np).

Thomas, W.P. and Collier, V.P. (1997) *School Effectiveness for Language Minority Students*. Washington, DC: National Clearinghouse for English Language Acquisition.

Turkan, S., de Oliveira, L.C., Lee, O. and Phelps, G. (2014) Proposing a knowledge base for teaching academic content to English language learners: Disciplinary linguistic knowledge. *Teachers College Record* 116, 1–30.

US English (2018) See https://www.usenglish.org/ (accessed 1 March 2019).

Valdés, G. (1997) Dual-language immersion programs: A cautionary note concerning the education of language-minority students. *Harvard Educational Review* 67 (3), 391–430.

Index